Celebrate!
CHRISTMAS

EDITED BY EUGENE T. AND MARILYNN C. SULLIVAN

A delicious decoration!
Directions, page 49

PUBLISHED BY WILTON ENTERPRISES, INC., WOODRIDGE, ILLINOIS 60517

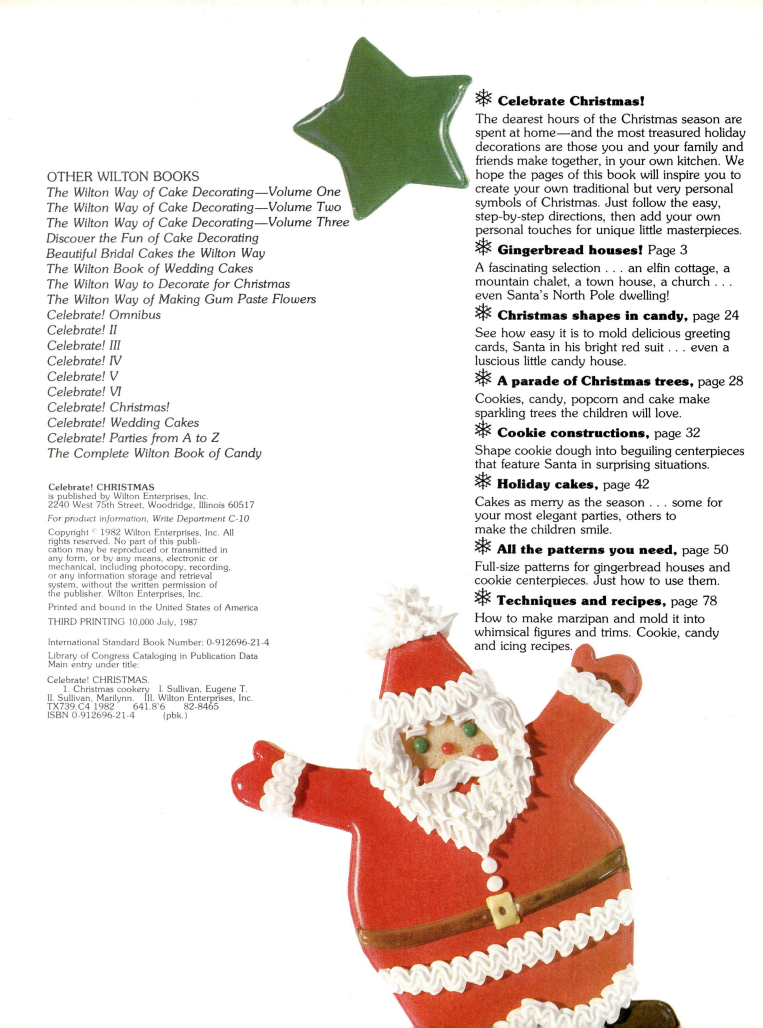

OTHER WILTON BOOKS

Celebrate! CHRISTMAS
is published by Wilton Enterprises, Inc.
2240 West 75th Street, Woodridge, Illinois 60517

For product information, Write Department C-10

Printed and bound in the United States of America

THIRD PRINTING 10,000 July, 1987

International Standard Book Number: 0-912696-21-4

Library of Congress Cataloging in Publication Data
Main entry under title:

Celebrate! CHRISTMAS.
     1. Christmas cookery   I. Sullivan, Eugene T.
II. Sullivan, Marilynn.   III. Wilton Enterprises, Inc.
TX739.C4 1982   641.8'6   82-8465
ISBN 0-912696-21-4   (pbk.)

❄ Celebrate Christmas!

The dearest hours of the Christmas season are
spent at home—and the most treasured holiday
decorations are those you and your family and
friends make together, in your own kitchen. We
hope the pages of this book will inspire you to
create your own traditional but very personal
symbols of Christmas. Just follow the easy,
step-by-step directions, then add your own
personal touches for unique little masterpieces.

❄ Gingerbread houses! Page 3

A fascinating selection . . . an elfin cottage, a
mountain chalet, a town house, a church . . .
even Santa's North Pole dwelling!

❄ Christmas shapes in candy, page 24

See how easy it is to mold delicious greeting
cards, Santa in his bright red suit . . . even a
luscious little candy house.

❄ A parade of Christmas trees, page 28

Cookies, candy, popcorn and cake make
sparkling trees the children will love.

❄ Cookie constructions, page 32

Shape cookie dough into beguiling centerpieces
that feature Santa in surprising situations.

❄ Holiday cakes, page 42

Cakes as merry as the season . . . some for
your most elegant parties, others to
make the children smile.

❄ All the patterns you need, page 50

Full-size patterns for gingerbread houses and
cookie centerpieces. Just how to use them.

❄ Techniques and recipes, page 78

How to make marzipan and mold it into
whimsical figures and trims. Cookie, candy
and icing recipes.

❄ Gingerbread Houses

Creating the house is just as much fun as viewing the magnificent final effect! Even though you start with the same pattern, your gingerbread house will be one of a kind. Once the house is assembled, don't spare the candy, cookie and swirling icing trims! Add decorative little figures, landscape with evergreens, light the windows! The pictures that follow will give you lots of ideas—your own imagination will make your little holiday house unique!

Building a gingerbread house is best done as a team effort. So gather your family and friends in the kitchen to begin this fascinating job. When you sniff the glorious scents from the oven, you'll know that Christmas is near!

❄ *Above:* a cosy cottage is set in an evergreen grove. For details and a view of a very different house made from the same pattern, turn the page.

 ## An elfin cottage

This enchanting little cottage looks like it was baked in a kitchen in Germany, where gingerbread houses originated. If you've never made a gingerbread house, this is an ideal one to begin with. Not counting the cookie trims, there are only six main pieces that go together very quickly. Read through the directions below, and study pages 6 and 7 for basic methods—then begin your own festive little cookie cottage.

We trimmed the roof with brightly colored cookies, studded the front door with candies and placed two little plastic elves in the front yard. You may decide on a completely different decorating scheme and achieve just as charming an effect.

Upper base is a 10″ circle of gingerbread, lower base is 12″ in diameter. Floor plan measures about 7½″ wide x 4″.

Day one: bake pieces and prepare base

Prepare patterns, then make a recipe of Grandma's Gingerbread (page 80). Divide dough in fourths and work with one fourth at a time. Roll out dough to about ⅛″ thickness on the back of a lightly oiled cookie sheet. (Place damp towel beneath cookie sheet so it will not shift.) Cut wall sections first, tracing patterns accurately with a sharp knife. Cut upper base by using a 10″ cake circle, pan or plate as a pattern.

Roll out dough a little thinner on separate cookie sheet and cut out roof sections. Finally, roll dough as thin as possible and cut tiny cookies for trim with miniature cutters, door and chimney pieces. Note that the chimney has an unusual triangular shape. Bake all pieces as recipe directs, cool on wire racks, then crisp overnight on cookie sheets.

Cover a double 12″ cardboard cake circle with foil to use for lower base.

Day two: construct the cottage

Study the directions on page 6, and make a batch of royal icing (page 80) to use as glue. Secure gingerbread upper base to lower base.

First, construct the chimney on wax paper and set aside to dry. Determine position of house on base and mark a line to indicate back wall. Now construct side walls, front wall, then roof as shown on page 6. Add chimney last, short side resting on ridge of roof.

Take out a little of the icing from the batch and thin with corn syrup. Brush the icing over the tiny cookies with a pastry brush, then sprinkle thickly with tinted crystal sugar while the icing is still wet.

Day three: add the trim

Review the general directions on page 7, then cover all seams (except ridge of roof) with candy. Decorate door, then attach it and all cookie and candy trims to side walls. Use royal icing for glue.

Make a batch of boiled icing (page 80) and swirl over the roof for snow. Immediately sprinkle with edible glitter. Press in candies on ridge. Add miniature cookies to roof, stroking a little more icing on backs if needed.

Swirl snow on gingerbread base, sprinkle with glitter and set the little elves in place. Press in candy wafers for path. Make a fence of miniature pretzels, securing each with a dab of icing. With a small spatula, stroke icing snow over tops of candy and cookie trims, and on fence. Complete your little scene by attaching a border of candies around upper base.

Another version *shown on page 3*

If you like to create piped designs with a decorating tube, you can show off your skill on a little cottage like this. Do all piping with tube 2 and boiled icing (page 80). Patterns are the same as those used for the Elfin Cottage.

In addition to all house pieces, bake about two dozen rectangular cookies, about 1″ x 1½″, cut from thinly rolled dough. These will be used for eaves. Center each with an almond before baking. Also bake two tiny gingerbread figures and a street sign.

After the cottage is assembled, cover all seams with beading. Pipe beading to edge door and windows, and to form wreath on door. Decorate the gingerbread figures and street sign.

Ice the roof smoothly. Attach assembled chimney and cover it with piped lattice. Trim roof with candies, arranged in flower patterns, securing with dots of icing. Pipe curving stems and leaves, then attach small cookies for eaves. Complete candy trim, then pull out "icicles", using thinned icing.

Ice upper base, then set figures in position on mounds of icing. Attach street sign, propping with a toothpick. Complete the scene with piped evergreen trees (page 31). Sift a little confectioners' sugar over them for "snow", then attach candies for border. As a final touch, add two little plastic doves.

Build a gingerbread house

It's easy to build a gingerbread house, and it's a project that family and friends will have fun sharing. In this book we've divided the construction of the house into three stages. On *day one,* cut and bake the pieces of the house, and allow them to dry thoroughly overnight. *Day two,* construct the house. On *day three,* decorate. Shop ahead of time for candy and any ingredients you may need for gingerbread, cookies or icing. Recipes are on page 80.

❄ Day one: bake pieces and make base

1. Transfer patterns as described on page 50. Mix a batch of Grandma's Gingerbread (page 80). Form it into a rough ball shape and cut in fourths. You will work with one fourth at a time, so wrap the rest tightly in plastic wrap. Lightly oil the backs of several 12″ x 18″ cookie sheets (the kind with sides about 1″ high). Lay one oiled cookie sheet, upside down, on a damp towel. This will keep the cookie sheet from shifting. Lay a fourth of the gingerbread batch on the cookie sheet, pat to form a rough rectangle, then roll it out with a rolling pin lightly dusted with flour.

For wall sections, roll out to about ⅛″ thickness, *for roof sections,* roll slightly thinner. *For small details,* roll the dough as thin as possible.

2. Cut out wall sections first. Lay prepared patterns lightly on rolled-out dough and cut around edges with sharp knife. Pick up the scraps around cut pieces and wrap in plastic to reroll later. Continue rolling out dough and cutting out pieces on oiled cookie sheets, making sure to keep walls, roof and small pieces on separate cookie sheets. Bake separately, too, in a preheated 350° F oven. Thinner pieces require less baking time than thicker ones.

Transfer to wire baking racks with a large spatula. After all pieces are baked, check with patterns to make sure you have all the pieces needed to build your house. Allow to cool. Lay on cookie sheets covered with paper towels to crisp completely, overnight.

3. Every house needs both an upper and lower base. (The sizes will be noted in directions for each house.) *Start with the lower base.* Make it of two thicknesses of corrugated cardboard. Use cake circles or boards, or cut from a corrugated carton with a sharp knife. Place the two cardboards together, grains running in opposite directions for rigidity. Press masking tape all around the edges. Cover this lower base with foil, cut about 1½″ larger on all sides than the cardboard. Lay base on foil and fold the foil edges smoothly over the cardboard. Tape in place. *The upper base* may be made of corrugated cardboard, gingerbread or 1″ thick styrofoam. If you choose cardboard or styrofoam, ice with royal icing, then dry.

To attach the two bases, stroke five or six dabs of royal icing on lower base, center upper base over it and press gently. Dry.

❄ Day two: construct the house

1. Use royal icing as "glue" to attach all sections. First construct chimney, gable or any other small detail separately on wax paper. Fit a decorating cone with tube 3 or 4 and fill with royal icing. For a chimney, pipe a line of icing on one side, then set second side against it. Pipe icing on second side and add third side. Continue with fourth side. Hold pieces in place a minute until icing sets, then dry upside down. Do other details the same way.

Prop walls upright with jars or cans until set

First build chimney on wax paper and dry

Attach chimney and other details to constructed house

2. To determine the position of the house on the base, cut a piece of paper to the measurements of the "floor plan". (This will be given with directions for each house.) Lay the paper on the base. Most houses are set back on the base to allow more room in the front. With a pin, draw a line to mark the position of the back wall.

3. Fit a decorating cone with tube 7 or 8, fill with royal icing. Pipe a thick line of icing on the marked line and set back wall in position. Pipe icing on base and one side of a side wall and set in position against back wall. Repeat for second side wall. Finally add front wall. A helper is very useful to hold one wall section as you add a second. Reinforce the wall joinings by adding lines of piping to the inside of the house. Use straight-sided jars or cans to hold walls upright until the icing sets.

4. To attach the roof, pipe a line of icing on top of back wall and rear edges of side walls. Carefully position one roof section on rear of house. Have a helper hold it as you pipe icing on top edges of roof and remaining walls. Place second roof section in position. Pipe icing on outside ridge of roof to reinforce it. Finally attach chimney by piping a line of icing around base and gently pressing in position. Make sure it is vertical by adding more icing on one side, if needed. Keep roof propped until it dries thoroughly, at least several hours.

5. *Gingerbread tips.* Assembly is easier if the sides of walls are straightened. Use a metal-edged ruler to indicate straight line on side edge of wall. Score gently and repeatedly with a sharp knife until wall is trimmed.

Small details, such as chimneys, sometimes look neater if pieces are straightened. Lay pattern on baked pieces to determine shape, then trim as above.

If icing squishes out as you assemble pieces, don't be concerned. It will be hidden by piping or candy trim.

For pieces that accurately hold the shape of the pattern, place cookie sheet holding rolled-out dough in freezer for about five minutes. Then cut out pieces and bake.

❄ Day three: decorate your house

This is the most fun! Remember: work from top down and from the house itself outward to edge of base.

1. Cover seams. If you are using candy, pipe a dot of royal icing on candy and gently press to seam. For tiny candies, pipe a line of royal icing on the seam, then quickly press the candies in position. Do not add candies to the ridge of the roof at this time. If you decide to cover the seams with piping, do it now, using royal icing.

2. Trim door then attach by piping a line of icing around edges on reverse side and pressing to house. Now attach windows and any other trim to side walls with royal icing.

3. Add a fresh fall of snow to roof and ground. Make a batch of boiled icing (page 80) and swirl over the roof with a spatula. Pull points from roof edge to look like icicles.

For a sparkly touch, immediately sprinkle with edible glitter. Now press in candies on the ridge of the roof while icing is still damp.

Swirl icing over the ground area, bringing it to edge of upper base, and banking it up against the walls of the house. Sprinkle with glitter, then press in candies for path.

Now add bushes, trees, figures or any other details.

4. Stroke a little icing "snow" on tops of door, windows, trees and bushes with a small spatula. For a final touch, add a border of candies, attached by piping a dot of icing on each. Or pipe a royal icing border.

❄ How to light a gingerbread house

1. Prepare upper and lower bases for your house as described on page 6. The upper base should be cut from 1″ thick styrofoam for strength. Cut a piece of paper the size and shape of the floor plan of your house and lay on upper base to indicate position of the house. Trace this rectangle with a pin. Cut a hole about 1″ in diameter in the center of the rectangle. It's easiest to do this with a small cookie cutter. Center the upper base over the cardboard lower base and trace the hole. Cut it out with a sharp knife. Now assemble the two bases with royal icing. Dry.

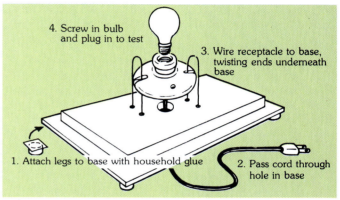

2. Glue four 1″ high legs to the underside of the base, setting them about 1½″ in from the edges. Plastic stud plates made for cake separator sets are ideal—or you can use sugar cubes or spools.

3. Fit a porcelain bulb receptacle with a two-strand electrical cord. Attach a plug to the other end. Set the receptacle on the base, drawing the cord through the hole below. Wire the receptacle to the base with light florist's wire, passing the wire through both bases. Make holes for wire with a nail. Screw in a 15-watt bulb. Plug in to test.

4. Now build the walls of your house around the receptacle, just as directed on page 6. Before putting on the roof, cut a piece of foil to correspond to the floor area of the house. Cut a hole in the center and place it over the receptacle, smoothing it in place on the floor of the house. This will make the light seem brighter.

❄ How to store your gingerbread house

Your fanciful little Christmas house may be stored for several years if carefully wrapped and protected from heat, light and moisture.

Roll down the sides of a large lightweight plastic bag. (A dry cleaner's bag is ideal.) Set the house in the bag and carefully pull up the sides.

Seal with a twist tie. For added protection, box the wrapped house in a sturdy cardboard carton. With a sharp knife, cut two corners of the box down to the base. Slide the house into the box and tape the corners of the box together. Store in a cool dry place.

Hansel and Gretel discover the witch's cottage

The roof is covered with luscious pink icing, the walls are studded with candy and the trees and flowers are candy, too. Even the witch's oven is made of sugar! Build this fairytale house of gingerbread and let light beam through the hard candy windows. Upper base is 12″ x 14″ wide, lower base is 14″ x 16″ wide, floor plan is 6″ x 7¾″ wide.

❄ Day one: bake gingerbread, prepare base and candy

Make a batch of gingerbread (page 80), roll out and cut pieces as described on page 6. Bake and cool overnight. Also bake Hansel and Gretel, using boy and girl cutters from Christmas Set. Prepare bases, using styrofoam for upper base if you wish to light your house. See pages 6 and 7.

Mold hard candy lollipops for trees and small hearts and shapes for windows. Recipe and directions, page 80.

❄ Day two: assemble cottage, mold oven

Page 6 shows you how. First put together the three-piece gable and the chimney on wax paper. Dry upside down. Pipe a line of royal icing around opening for front window and press on molded hard candy shape. Do the same for other window openings, using molded shapes and hearts.

Now mark the position of the back wall on base, placing it about 1½″ from back edge and centering from side to side. Construct walls, then add roof. When roof has set about 30 minutes, attach gable, then chimney. Pipe a line of icing around pointed front edge of gable and press on gable trim. Dry overnight.

Sugar mold the oven (page 80) using Small Wonder Mold pan as mold. Sprinkle with edible glitter and dry.

❄ Day three: decorate the cottage

Decorate Hansel and Gretel with tube 1 and tinted royal icing. Make a batch of boiled icing (page 80). Ice chimney thickly and cover with candy wafers. On side of house, directly below chimney, mark a strip with a pin, the width of the chimney. Use a spatula to fill in with icing, then cover with wafers. Ice roof, gable sides and door. Add all candy trim. Ice top of upper base and roughen with a spatula for "grass." Attach door in open position, then secure sugar oven. Landscape the grounds with lollipop trees and gumdrop flowers on toothpick stems. Attach Hansel and Gretel with dots of icing, then make a jellybean border around upper base. Light it up—then watch the children's smiles!

Construct chimney and gable and dry upside down on wax paper.

Attach hard candy windows before constructing walls. Add roof, then gable, then chimney. Attach gable trim.

❄ The beautiful Christmas Crèche

The heart of Christmas is the crèche. Create it, simply and reverently, in gingerbread. It will grace your home at the holidays and give everyone who sees it a feeling of sweetness and peace. This little crèche is very easy to construct because cookie cutters do much of the work. Figures, trees, star and heart-shaped openings in the stable are all simply stamped out with cutters. Upper base is 11" x 16" corrugated cardboard, lower base 13" x 18".

❄ Day one: bake pieces, prepare base

Consult pages 6 and 7 for basic procedures. All gingerbread is rolled to ⅛" thickness. Cut floor, roof and walls, then cut heart-shaped openings in walls with cutters from Miniature and Heart Cutter sets. Mary, Joseph and the Infant are cut with the Gingerbread cutter set. Trim off flare of skirt from figure of Joseph. Angels, trees and star are cut with cutters from Christmas set. Cut four trees, then cut two of them in half, vertically. Allow all pieces to crisp overnight.

❄ Day two: construct stable, decorate cookies

First attach floor to base with royal icing. Place it 2¼" in from back of base, centering from side to side. Construct walls, first back, then sides, around stable floor. Pipe a line of icing around tops of walls and add roof. Construct manger.

Pipe tube 1 beading around heart-shaped openings in walls. Use the same tube for trim on star and figures. Pipe radiating lines on small circle for halo. Pipe tube 4 bulbs to cover seams. Now attach roof braces and allow to dry overnight.

❄ Day three: complete decoration

Attach two bases to back of Mary—do the same for Joseph. Pipe straw on manger with tube 233, then press on halo and Infant. Attach star to front edge of roof. Secure whole tree to side wall, lining up center of tree and rear edge of wall. Pipe a thick line of icing down center of tree, then press on two half-tree sections. Edge outer branches with tube 13 shells. Do the same on second wall. Pipe lines of icing down centers of backs of angels and secure to front walls.

Stroke boiled icing "snow" on roof and ground and sprinkle with edible glitter. Set figures in position. Finish with a tube 19 shell border around upper base.

Attach two braces to backs of Mary and Joseph

Secure whole tree to side wall, then attach two half-trees

 **Santa sets out...**

on his annual night-long journey. Mrs. Claus and jolly elves wave him on his way. His cosy house has a scarlet roof, door and shutters, hard candy windows permit a glimpse of the sparkly Christmas tree inside. There's even a mailbox at the front dooryard! Make all the charming figures from marzipan—pages 78 and 79 give the easy directions.

Upper base is 10" x 14" wide, lower base 12" x 16". Floor area is 5½" x 10½".

❄ Day one: bake pieces, prepare candy and make marzipan

Cut out and bake roof, shutters and door from Roll-out dough (page 80) tinted red. Use gingerbread for walls and balcony. Prepare base (pages 6 and 7) and electrify. To make "glass" for windows, trace window openings on foil, then oil foil. Make a recipe of hard candy (page 80). As soon as it has cooked, spoon hot syrup over traced openings, letting syrup extend about ¼" beyond tracings. Mold a tree-shaped lollipop for tree. Start construction of marzipan figures.

❄ Day two: assemble house with royal icing

1. To make balcony, trim six thin pretzels to 1" length. Assemble with balcony floor on wax paper as diagram shows. Add more pretzels for railing. Attach balcony braces. Build chimney on wax paper.

2. Trim lollipop tree with tube 2 balls. Attach candy window glass by piping a line of icing around openings on wrong side of walls. Press candy in position. Pipe window panes with tube 1s. Attach balcony to front of house. Attach shutters.

3. Construct walls, then cut off stick on lollipop tree to 1½" and push into base behind front window. Add roof, then chimney. Complete marzipan figures and model mailbox.

❄ Day three: add finishing touches

Pipe chimney, door and shutter trim with tube 1. Attach door. Drop tube 13 strings for garlands on balcony, then cover with tube 2 needles. Pipe wreath with tube 65s, then add tube 1 bows. Add candy trim to cover seams. Finally, stroke boiled icing snow over roof and ground, sprinkle with glitter and set the marzipan figures in the front yard. Secure mailbox to base, then add a border of miniature marshmallows. Light up your little tableau! It will be the center of attention all through the holidays.

Clip pretzels to 1" length and ice to balcony floor for posts. Add more pretzels for railings.

Ice braces to wrong side of balcony floor.

 A quaint Swiss chalet

This cosy alpine dwelling has a steeply pitched and angled roof, easily constructed in gingerbread. Soft light beams through the hard candy windows, decorated with dainty piping. We completed our chalet with lollipop trees, piped bushes and a scarlet weathervane—use your own bright ideas to decorate your creation.

Upper base is 12″ x 14″ wide, lower base 14″ x 16″, floor area of house is about 7″ square.

❄ Day one: bake pieces, prepare details

Review pages 6 and 7 for basic procedures. Prepare patterns and a recipe of Grandma's Gingerbread (page 80). Cut walls and doorsteps ⅛″ thick, roof sections from thinner dough, chimney and door from dough rolled as thin as possible. Bake all pieces and dry overnight. Use hard candy recipe (page 80) to mold about 8 daisies and half a dozen small lollipops for trees. Cut upper base from 1″ thick styrofoam, lower base from double cardboard covered with foil. Attach electric fixture (page 7).

❄ Day two: assemble the chalet

Make a second recipe of hard candy to secure "daisy" windows. After syrup has finished cooking, place pan in a larger pan of very hot water. With the tip of a teaspoon, dribble hot candy around window openings of wall pieces and immediately cover with molded daisies. To make icicles, dribble lines of hot candy on oiled foil. Paint chimney pieces, door and door steps with royal icing thinned with water. When dry, pipe freehand trim on chimney and windows with tube 1s and royal icing. Use tube 2 to pipe wreath on door. To make royal icing weathervane, tape pattern to cardboard and tape wax paper smoothly over it. Paint a toothpick with thinned icing and lay on wax paper for post. Outline pattern with tube 1, then fill in with thinned icing.

Pipe bushes as described on page 31.

Assemble chimney separately, then walls and roof. Attach upper roof pieces first, then lower pieces. Add chimney, doorsteps, then door in slightly open position.

❄ Day three: decorate and landscape the chalet

Trim walls and cover all seams with candy. Attach icicles to roof edges with dabs of royal icing. Swirl boiled icing "snow" on roof and sprinkle with edible glitter. Push in weather vane and add candies to ridge of roof. Swirl snow on upper base, add candy path and sprinkle with glitter.

Arrange bushes and lollipop trees around chalet, then attach a candy border all around upper base.

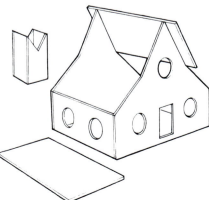

Construct chimney separately. Attach windows and trim to walls, then build on base. Attach upper roof pieces first, then lower roof pieces.

Complete construction with chimney, doorsteps and door.

A stylish Victorian brownstone

If you're a city dweller, you'll delight in this townhouse in the style of 100 years ago. Lofty arched windows, an elaborate cornice and high front stairs make it very authentic. Rolled marzipan makes it easy to create all the colorful trim.

Upper base is 10″ square, lower base 12″ square. Floor area of house is about 6″ square. Refer to pages 6 and 7 for basic procedures, page 80 for gingerbread and icing recipes.

Would you like to make a replica of your own house? You can build a gingerbread house in almost any architectural style. To make your own patterns, take careful measurements of the outside of your house. Translate feet to inches, then divide by four. For example: if your house is 24 feet wide, translate to 24 inches, divide by four to equal 6 inches. Your pattern will be 6″ wide. Note details carefully, then reproduce them in candy, icing or marzipan. You'll create a charming little double of your home to display at Christmas time.

❆ Day one: bake pieces, prepare marzipan

Cut all gingerbread pieces and bake as recipe directs. Make sure stairs are cut from gingerbread ¼″ thick. For accurate shapes, cut stairs in one strip as pattern indicates, but *do not remove surrounding scraps.* Bake, then re-cut shapes with a sharp knife. Cool gingerbread on racks, then lay on paper towel-covered cookie sheets to crisp overnight. Make a recipe of marzipan (page 78) and divide in thirds. You will be using only ⅓ of the recipe, so wrap the remainder tightly in plastic wrap and refrigerate for another purpose. Tint half of your ⅓ portion red, the remainder blue. Roll out blue marzipan and cut windows. Cut door, bay window roof and supports from red. For chimney, form a 1″ cylinder from remaining red marzipan. Lay on flat surface and flatten with a ruler to ½″ thickness. Trim sides to 1¼″ width. Lay all marzipan pieces on paper towels to dry and harden overnight, then glaze.

❆ Day two: assemble house

For a neat, trim effect, all windows, cornice and door are attached to front of house and trimmed before walls are assembled.

1. Build stairway first. Starting at bottom, stack all steps, lining up at back and sides and securing with royal icing. Lay assembled stairway on front of house, left side of stairway about ¼″ from left side of house, bottom of stairway and front of house aligned. With a pin, mark a line where top step meets house. Remove stairway.

2. Attach gingerbread cornice, then top with marzipan cornice. Attach red door, bottom of door on marked line. Attach fanlight above it. Now draw a line with a pin to indicate center of house, from top to bottom. Attach main floor window beside door, center on marked center line, top lining up with top of fanlight. Now attach remaining front windows, using first window as guide for even spacing. Attach windows to bay window sides. Using royal icing, indicate panes and door panels with tube 1, frames with tube 3, and window sills with tube 83. Trim cornice with tube 1 scallops and dots, then add tube 13 shells.

3. Construct side panels of bay window on gingerbread base, then attach bay window top. Clip ten toothpicks to 1½″ length for railing posts. Cover with thinned royal icing by inserting into a decorating cone fitted with tube 5, using light pressure as you draw out.

4. Mark a line for position of back wall of house on base, then construct walls. Attach stairway just below door. Add roof. Pipe lines of icing on edges of bay window and gently press to side of house. Hold a few minutes until set.

❆ Day three: finish decorating house

Pipe tube 13 shells on top and corner seams. Pipe wreaths and garlands with tube 1, add red bows with same tube. Pipe a mound of icing on top of bay window, then add three-piece marzipan roof. Attach base support the same way. Trim with tube 13. Attach chimney, trimming at base to correspond to slanted roof.

With tip of a small pointed knife, make holes in steps to receive posts. Use tube 1 to fill holes with royal icing, then insert posts. Drop a tube 1 string from post to post to make railing.

Make a batch of boiled icing and stroke over roof for snow. Sprinkle with edible glitter. Do the same on the ground. Plant gum drops and mint leaf candies for bushes. With a small spatula, pull out icicles and tiny snow drifts from roof and window frames.

We added a little snowman in the front court yard. Figure pipe him ahead of time with tube 2A and boiled icing. Arms are toothpicks, features and buttons are piped with tube 1, hat with tube 364.

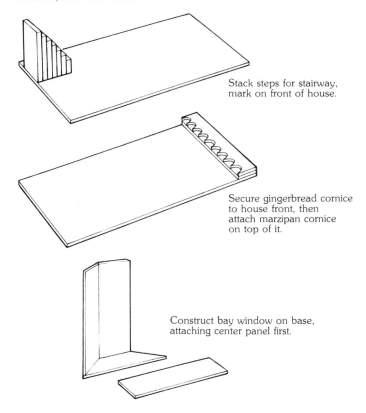

Stack steps for stairway, mark on front of house.

Secure gingerbread cornice to house front, then attach marzipan cornice on top of it.

Construct bay window on base, attaching center panel first.

A glowing village church . . .

makes an exquisite centerpiece for the holidays. This little church is easy to construct from gingerbread and the soft light beaming through hard candy windows gives a very dramatic effect. Consult pages 6 and 7 for basic procedure, page 80 for all recipes.

Make upper base of styrofoam, 10″ square, lower base 12″ square. Floor area is about 6″ square.

❄ Day one: bake pieces, prepare base, candy

Make a batch of Grandma's gingerbread and cut all pieces, using patterns. Roll out the dough as thin as possible to cut all pieces for steeple. To make it easy to construct, place cookie sheet containing cut-out pieces in the freezer for five minutes before baking. *Do not remove scraps,* but bake, then immediately re-cut the pieces with a sharp knife. Prepare the base, using styrofoam for upper base, and attach electric fixture.

To mold the diamond-shaped windows, trace eight or more window openings on foil. Oil the foil. As soon as hard candy has cooked, spoon a little candy over each traced diamond, letting it spread ¼″ or more beyond tracing. Allow to harden. Mold the "rose window" in a daisy mold.

❄ Day two: construct the church

1. Attach diamond windows to inside of walls by piping a line of royal icing around window opening, then pressing on hard candy "glass". Pipe a line of icing around round opening on outside of steeple and press on daisy shape. Use tube 1s to pipe meandering lines of cornelli on diamond window glass. Pipe freehand designs around all windows with tube 1s.

2. Take out a little icing, thin with water, tint red and paint door. When dry, pipe tube 1s beading. Pipe tube 13 shells on wax paper to form cross. Make tree from candy as shown on page 31.

3. Assemble steeple peak on steeple cover and set aside to dry. Now construct walls, then roof and prop until set.

4. Hold steeple lower sides against front of church to see if they fit under roof. Trim as necessary. Lay steeple front, face down, on wax paper and attach steeple lower sides. When dry, attach to front of church. Now hold steeple upper sides and back in position on roof to check for fit. Trim as necessary. Now attach steeple upper sides and back to roof and steeple front, attaching sides first.

Pipe a line of icing on top of steeple and set steeple point in position. Attach door and cross with royal icing. Allow assembled church to dry overnight.

❄ Day three: decorate the church

Cover seams with tube 13 shells, using royal icing. Pipe shells and tube 2 dots below steeple cover. Cover roof with candy wafers, working from bottom up and overlapping rows of wafers. Add a jellybean foundation.

Now make a batch of boiled icing and stroke over roof, then ground. Sprinkle with edible glitter. Press in candies on ridge of roof. Add candy path and bushes. Set tree in position. With a small spatula, add more snow on bushes, tree and ridge of roof. Your beautiful little church is complete. Plug it in and watch light stream through the windows.

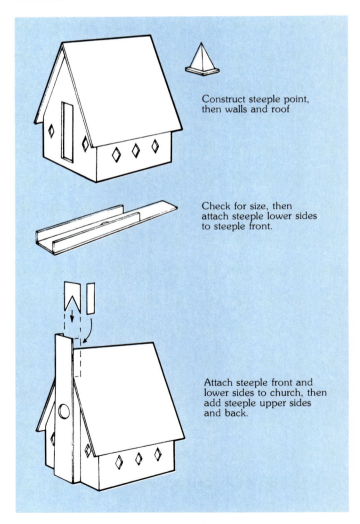

Construct steeple point, then walls and roof

Check for size, then attach steeple lower sides to steeple front.

Attach steeple front and lower sides to church, then add steeple upper sides and back.

A snug farmhouse

Create an old-fashioned country scene with the charm of a three-dimensional Christmas card! The roofs are made of tinted Roll-out cookie dough, the walls from gingerbread and the windows from hard candy. Review pages 6 and 7 for basic procedure. All recipes are on page 80. Upper styrofoam base is 12″ x 15″ wide, lower base 14″ x 17″, floor plan, including porches, about 7½″ x 9″.

❄ Day one: bake pieces, prepare base, windows

Make a recipe of Roll-out cookie dough and one of gingerbread. Cut off about one-third of the Roll-out dough (save the rest for another purpose). Tint a very small portion red for doors. Tint remainder blue for roofs and window trims. Cut walls, chimney and porch floor from gingerbread. For accurately shaped pieces, cut pieces, then chill and *bake without removing scraps.* As soon as removed from oven, re-cut with a sharp knife.

Prepare base and install lighting. Make hard candy windows as described on page 12. Mold a tree-shaped lollipop. Decorate with tube 2.

❄ Day two: assemble house, prepare details

Attach "glass" to backs of window openings. Construct chimney. Follow diagram for order of wall construction. Clip stick on lollipop tree to 1½″ and push into base behind front window. Attach long roof sections to back and right side of house. Add short roof sections. Attach chimney. Pipe evergreen tree and bushes (page 31).

❄ Day three: add finishing touches

Pipe window and door frames with tube 4. Pipe tube 1 panes, tube 83 window sills. Attach triangular window trims. Pipe tube 1 wreaths, tube 3 bulbs to cover seams.

Construct porch. Clip four candy canes to 3½″ length. Pipe a tube 5 line of icing as marked on walls for front porch roof. Lay roof on this line. Have a helper hold it as you pipe a dot of icing on top and bottom of one candy cane piece and set it on porch floor to support roof. Attach side porch roof and remaining candy cane supports the same.

For lightning rods, clip thin florists' wire into 2″ pieces. Fit a decorating cone with tube 5, and insert wire into tube. As you apply light pressure, pull out wire and stick into styrofoam to dry. Pipe tube 4 balls, then clip to 1¼″.

Swirl boiled icing "snow" on roofs and ground and sprinkle with edible glitter. Insert lightning rods. Clip thin pretzels to 1¼″ length and build woodpile. Position bushes and tree and add a little snowman. (See page 16)

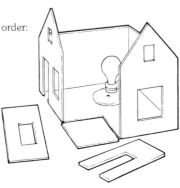

Construct walls in this order:
1. Long back wall
2. Long side wall
3. Pointed side wall
4. Pointed front wall
5. Front porch floor
6. Front porch walls

 **An angelic choir**

Eight little angels sing around a lighted pavillion crowned with a rosy roof! All through the holidays this centerpiece will charm your guests and delight the children!

Windows are molded from hard candy, walls are gingerbread, roof and angels are cut from tinted cookie dough. Recipes are on page 80.

❄ Day one: bake pieces, prepare base, candy

Tint one-half of the recipe for Roll-out cookies a delicate pink. (Save rest for another purpose.) Cut out eight angels, using cutter from Christmas set. Add more food color to tint remainder of dough a deeper pink and cut out roof sections. Cut walls, base and roof support from gingerbread.

Use two 14″ circles of corrugated cardboard to make base. Cover with foil and attach legs and electric fixture (see directions on page 7).

Make a recipe of hard candy, tint, and mold eight star shapes and eight daisies for windows.

❄ Day two: construct pavillion

1. Pipe a tube 3 line of royal icing around circular opening in a roof section. Attach molded daisy. Continue with remaining roof sections. Attach molded star shapes to wall sections the same way.

2. Construct roof. As a temporary support, cut point off an ice cream cone, bringing cone to a height of 3¾″. Cover with wax paper and tape to center of a stiff board. Lay roof support on board. Pipe a tube 7 line of icing on bottom of one roof section and attach to roof support, point resting on ice cream cone. Pipe icing on side and bottom edges of second roof section and attach to first. Continue until roof is complete.

3. Construct walls. Attach gingerbread base to cardboard base with royal icing. Pipe a tube 7 line of icing on bottom of one wall section. Set on base. Pipe a line of icing on side and bottom of second wall section and attach. Continue until walls are complete.

4. Pipe a line of icing around top of wall and set completed roof on it, making sure it is centered. Dry overnight.

❄ Decorate angels and pavillion

Pipe trim and features on angels with tube 1 and royal icing. Do hair with tube 13. When dry, turn over and attach a row of three miniature marshmallows to back of each, about ½″ up from bottom of skirt.

Pipe tube 14 shells to cover seams on wall and roof. Pipe zigzag garlands on edge of roof with tube 19. Begin with light pressure, build up to heavy pressure in center, then relax pressure as you near corner. Use the same tube to pipe upright shells on peak and corners of roof. Finish with rosettes at base. Attach angels by piping dots of icing on marshmallows. Light up the pavillion for a bit of Christmas magic!

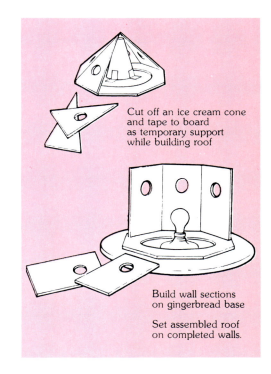

Cut off an ice cream cone and tape to board as temporary support while building roof

Build wall sections on gingerbread base

Set assembled roof on completed walls.

mold Christmas shapes in candy

A delicious little candy cottage

Every inch, from roof to snowy ground, is edible! This decorative little dwelling is made from confectionery coating, quickly molded in plastic molds. Pretty pink coating makes the roof, white the woodwork and yard, and chocolate-flavored coating the walls. Bushes and trees are molded, too.

❈ How to mold the house sections

1. *Work with one color of confectionery coating* at a time. Here are the approximate amounts you'll need.

> For pink roof and trim, about ¾ pound.
> For chocolate-flavored walls, about 1½ pounds.
> For white ground and trim, about 2 pounds.
> For green trees and chimney, about ½ pound.

By melting and molding these amounts, you will have some coating left over. This extra coating may be saved and used for another project.

2. *Melt confectionery coating* in a double boiler. Fill lower pan with water to a depth below level of top pan. Bring water to simmer, remove from heat. Fill top pan with coating (either wafers or chopped). Stir until coating is smooth and completely melted and at about 110°F—never more than 115°F. Use a low-temperature thermometer to check. Remove top pan from lower pan and continue stirring coating until temperature has cooled to about 103°F.

3. *Fill plastic molds* with melted coating, using a small ladle. When mold is filled, hold a few inches above surface and drop sharply several times to level and to eliminate air bubbles. Hold mold above eye level. If bubbles still remain, drop mold again.

4. *Chill by placing on freezer floor* until mold appears frosty. This will take about 20 minutes. If any dark areas still remain on mold, replace in freezer until entire mold appears frosty.

5. *Invert mold* and hold about an inch above towel-covered surface. Very gently flex or tap mold and candy will fall out.

❈ Add color contrast with flow-in method

Your little house will look more professional with contrasting color on woodwork, shutters and windows.

1. Place just five or six wafers each of yellow, pink and white coating in small glass jars. Place jars in a shallow pan of hot water. Stir with a popsicle stick until melted.

2. Fill a paper decorating cone with melted white coating.

(No more than half full.) Cut a tiny opening in the point of the cone. Using very light pressure, fill in any areas on the molds for the walls of the house that you would like white. Now do the same for pink shutters, then for yellow windows. Colors will set in just a few minutes.

3. Fill entire mold with melted chocolate-flavored coating. Drop mold to remove air bubbles, then chill and unmold.

❈ How to mold "yard" and bushes

For yard, use a 10″ square aluminum pan as mold. Pour in melted white confectionery coating to a depth of about ¼″. Chill and unmold as described above.

Mold trees in a tree-shaped lollipop mold. Place sticks in position on mold, pour in melted coating. Rotate sticks (this assures they remain firmly in the candy), then chill for about 20 minutes and unmold. For bushes, mold coating in tree-shaped bonbon molds, chilling for about eight minutes.

❈ Construct the cottage

Do this in much the same way that you would construct a gingerbread cottage (pages 6 and 7).

1. Cover a double 12″ square of corrugated cardboard with foil (see page 6). Attach molded base to it with a few strokes of melted coating. Mark a line 5″ long on base, about 2″ in from edge and centered from side to side.

2. Fill a parchment paper decorating cone no more than half full with melted confectionery coating. Cut a tiny opening from point. Pipe coating thickly on marked line on base, then set back wall of house on line. Pipe a line of icing on bottom and one side of a side wall. Set in position against back wall. Continue with other two walls. Reinforce walls by piping lines of melted coating on inside seams. Pipe coating on top edges of walls and gently press on roof sections. Hold until set. Pipe coating on ridge of roof.

3. Attach chimney and bushes with dots of melted coating. Clip sticks on lollipop trees and push into base. Trim ridge of roof and make path with small chocolate candies. Sprinkle edible glitter over all to add sparkle to the scene. Cut chocolate-flavored wafers in half, then attach as a border around upper base.

Would you like to learn more magic with confectionery coating? Read Chapter 3 in The Complete Wilton Book of Candy.

❄ Delicious good wishes

A greeting that tastes as good as it looks is a happy surprise at Christmas! Mold these edible cards quickly and easily in confectionery coating, using clear plastic molds—then send them off to delighted friends. Each greeting card takes about a half pound of coating. Melt the same amount for several letters.

Add the special touch of color contrast with the simple flow-in method—or pipe colorful trims.

❄ Enjoy the holidays!

Put four or five red, and the same number of yellow, confectionery coating wafers in small glass jars. Half-fill a shallow pan with hot water from the tap and set the jars in it. Stir with a popsicle stick or small spoon until melted and smooth.

Make a paper decorating cone and fill with the melted red coating. Cut a tiny opening in the point of the cone. Using light pressure, fill the area of the letters on the mold. Let

the red coating set up, just a few minutes, while you fill a second cone with melted yellow coating. Cut point of cone and fill the area surrounding the letters, piping right on top of the red letters.

Now melt about ¾ pound of chocolate-flavored confectionery coating as described on page 24. Spoon into the mold right on top of colored areas. Drop the filled mold sharply several times to eliminate air bubbles. Place on floor of freezer for about 20 minutes. When outside of mold appears frosty all over, the candy is ready to be unmolded. Hold an inch or so above a towel-covered surface. Flex or gently tap mold and candy will fall out.

Melt just a few colored wafers in a small glass jar set in hot water. Spoon into a small paper decorating cone, cut a tiny opening in the point and sign your name.

❄ "Noël" and "Merry Christmas"

Use the same method that you used for "Enjoy" to add color to "Noël". First melt green confectionery coating in a small jar set in hot water. Fill a parchment decorating cone, cut point and flow in border of card, using light pressure on cone. Now flow in the letters "noë" and the accent on the candle flame in red melted coating. Melt a little yellow coating and fill the candle area. Fill the entire mold with chocolate-flavored coating, chill and unmold as described above. Sign your name with coating piped from a cone with tiny cut point.

"Merry Christmas" uses the same technique. First flow in green border and holly leaves. Add red berries and lettering. Finally, fill mold with white confectionery coating, chill and unmold.

❄ Christmas "love" in candy

Use plastic molds to shape the letters in confectionery coating, using the same melt-fill-chill method that you used for the greeting cards. Melt a few contrasting wafers in a small glass jar set in hot water. Place melted coating in a small parchment decorating cone, cut a tiny opening in the point and pipe the decorative hearts and dots. Box the letters and send to someone very special!

❄ Santa's here!

It's fun to mold this roly-poly saint in confectionery coating using a two-piece mold. Melt small amounts of pink, red and chocolate-flavored coatings in glass jars set in hot water. Flow in pink areas first, using a decorating cone with cut point as described for greeting cards.

Now flow in red areas on both halves of mold, making sure that coating goes well up over edges of molds. Do the same with chocolate-flavored coating.

Align the two halves of the mold, clip together and fill with melted white confectionery coating. You will need about five ounces. Prop filled mold with crumpled foil and chill in freezer for about 35 minutes. Take off clips, lay mold on its side and lift off upper half. If necessary, slip a dull knife between the two halves of the mold. Invert mold over surface, flex gently and Santa will fall out. Pipe his eyes with chocolate-flavored coating, smooth the seams with a small knife and he's ready for Christmas!

A parade of Christmas trees

A cookie tree . . .
easy to do,
pretty to view

Cake and candy make a centerpiece tree for your nicest party

Directions, page 31

A lollipop tree and a popcorn ball tree sparkle at Christmas parties!

30

Build a cookie tree

shown on page 28

It's just as easy as baking a batch of cookies—and the result is a spectacular 12″ Christmas tree! All you need is cookie dough and a set of star-shaped cutters.

❋ Day one: bake the cookies

You will need two batches of Roll-out cookies (page 80) for this big tree—some will be left over for another baking. Mix the batches separately, but tint at one time for a perfect match. Roll out on the backs of lightly oiled cookie sheets as described on page 6. Cut four cookies with each cutter.

❋ Day two: assemble the tree

First make a four-cookie pile of each size of cookie. Build the tree on a 6″ cake circle so you can move it easily to a serving tray. With a small spatula, put a dab of either royal or boiled icing on the circle and top it with the largest-size cookie. Add a second cookie, securing with icing, placing so points of star are at indentations of first star. Continue stacking the cookies with icing, changing the angle of each as you build. When you have used all four of the largest cookies, proceed to the next size smaller. At the very top of the tree, prop a smallest-size cookie upright with a toothpick. Spray the tree lightly with water (use a plant mister) and sprinkle with a shower of edible glitter.

A cake-and-candy tree

shown on page 29

Plan ahead and you can create this breathtaking centerpiece-dessert with ease!

❋ Day one: mold candy, prepare cake

1. Mold the letters in confectionery coating, using plastic molds. Add piped trim. (Pages 24 to 27 give directions.)

2. Bake a cake in an upright tree-shaped pan. Wrap tightly in plastic wrap and chill overnight.

3. Prepare base for your creation. Lower base is a double 12″ corrugated cardboard circle, upper base is a 10″ circle cut from 1″ thick styrofoam. Attach the two bases, then ice upper base with royal icing (page 80) and roughen with a spatula. Sprinkle with edible glitter.

❋ Day two: complete the tree

1. Secure cake to its base (this comes with the pan) with a mound of buttercream icing (page 43). Thin the icing and brush all over cake. Pipe "needles" with speedy tube 233. Use half-gumdrops for ornaments. Push in candle.

2. Mound royal icing in center of base and set completed tree on it. Attach molded letters to upper base with dots of royal icing. To serve tree to twelve, cut vertically in half. Lay halves, cut side down, on tray and slice.

A sparkling lollipop tree

Children will love this glittering tree! After it brightens the party table, pull out the lollipops for take-home treats. You will need about 150 purchased lollipops and a styrofoam cone, 9″ high. Ice the cone with royal icing. When dry, make marks with a pin from bottom to top every ¾″. Clip

lollipop sticks to 1½″ lengths. Starting at bottom, push sticks into tree on marked lines. As you near the top, you will need to clip the sticks shorter. We crowned our candy tree with a molded star lollipop.

A popcorn ball tree

Have a friend help you put this tree together in a jiffy! You'll need a 9″ styrofoam cone, iced with royal icing, and 21 popcorn balls, about 2½″ in diameter. As the popcorn balls are formed, press them against the iced cone in rows to form the tree. You'll need seven balls for bottom row, then rows of five, four and three balls. Crown with a single ball at the top. Work with the balls while they are still warm. Should they cool off, place in a low oven a few minutes.

To glaze completed tree, combine one cup of light corn syrup and two tablespoons of water. Bring to a boil, then brush over entire tree. Press candies into tree for trim.

Holiday popcorn balls

- 18 cups popped corn
- 1½ cups sugar
- 1½ cups light corn syrup
- ¾ cup water
- 3 tablespoons butter
- 3 teaspoons vanilla

Place popped corn in buttered bowls in oven set at lowest temperature.

1. Combine sugar, syrup and water in a three-quart heavy saucepan. Add butter, cut in thin slices. Place over medium heat and stir until all sugar crystals are dissolved. Wash down sides of pan with a pastry brush dipped in hot water. Clip on thermometer and continue cooking to 240°F. Remove from heat and stir in vanilla.

2. Pour syrup over the warmed popcorn and toss with two forks until evenly coated. When mixture is cool enough to handle, butter your hands and form into 2½″ balls.

❋ Trees for landscaping

For piped trees, cover an ice cream cone with royal icing. Starting at bottom, pull out "needles" with tube 74. *For bushes,* stick a toothpick into a marshmallow. Cover with icing, then pipe tube 74 needles, starting at bottom.

For candy trees, start with an iced ice cream cone. Cut candy spearmint leaves in half and attach to cone.

Cookie Constructions

Cookie dough, bright colors and your own imagination can make beguiling Christmas centerpieces. Turn the pages for creations that feature Santa in surprising situations!

 ## Santa-in-the-box

Tinted cookie dough put together in the "inlay" method makes it easy to create this delicious toy.

❆ Day one: cut and bake cookie pieces

1. You'll need just a half-recipe of Roll-out dough (page 80). Save rest for another purpose. Tint half of the dough red. From second half, take out a very small portion to leave untinted. From remainder, tint half yellow, half green. Roll out dough on backs of cookie sheets, using separate sheets for each color. As dough is rolled out, place in freezer for about five minutes before cutting. Prepare patterns.
From red dough, cut base of box, four 3" stars, two 1" hearts and Santa. Also, trace an 8" cake circle or plate for red base. *From yellow dough* cut two box sides, one box lid and two 1" stars. *From green dough,* cut two box sides, two 1" stars and one box lid. Cut a 1½" circle from untinted dough for Santa's face.

2. Use inlay method for color contrast. Lay cut-out red stars in star-shaped openings on box sides, cut-out red hearts in openings on lid. Fill round opening for Santa's face with untinted circle. Trim box sides by brushing backs of 1" stars with water, then centering on red stars. Cut circles with tube 12 for Santa's cheeks and a sliver for mouth. Brush backs with water and lay on face. Cut many yellow and green circles with tube 10, brush backs with water and lay on sides and lids of box for trim. Bake all pieces as recipe directs, Circle base will take about 20 minutes, other pieces less. Cool overnight.

3. Cover a double 10" cake circle with foil for base.

❆ Day two: assemble and decorate

1. Attach round cookie base to cardboard base with royal icing (page 80). Attach base of box to center of cookie base with icing.

2. Make a recipe of hard candy (page 80) to use as a strong "glue" to assemble box. When hard candy has cooked, place pan in a larger pan of simmering water. Working quickly, dip bottom of one side piece in hot candy and hold against box base an instant to harden. Dip one side and bottom of second side in candy, attach to first side. Continue with other two sides. Dip edges of lids in candy and set on box at an angle, as picture shows.

3. Decorate Santa. Use tube 13 and royal icing to pipe zigzag cuffs, mustache and beard. When dry, turn over and decorate other side so picture is complete from any angle.

Pipe tube 13 shells to cover seams on box, tube 17 shells around base. Pipe a mound of royal icing in bottom of base and set in Santa, propping with crumpled foil until dry. Fill box with candy. This cheery centerpiece will last for about a week—then eat it and enjoy!

 ## Tree-trim cookies

1. Stars and Shapes and Christmas Figure candy molds make charming tree trims. Roll out a small portion of gingerbread (page 80) about ½" thick. Dust molds with flour and firmly press small pieces of dough into depressions. Trim excess dough around edges. Tap mold, upside down, sharply on surface and cookie will fall out. Place on lightly oiled cookie sheet and place sheet in freezer for about ten minutes. Bake about ten minutes, until firm. As soon as cookies are taken from oven, cut a hole for hanging with tube 3. Cool on wire racks.

2. Decorate the cookies with tube 2 and royal icing as we did here—or leave them unadorned. Thread gold cord through holes to hang.

 ## Cookies, cake and lollipops!

Put them all together and you'll create this centerpiece—the ultimate in Christmas cheer! Cutters from the Christmas set speed the work along.

Would you like a recipe for a party that will be talked about until the next holiday season? Invite all the youngsters for their favorite fast food—pizza, fried chicken, hamburgers or hot dogs. Set the table with paper plates and this fabulous cookie construction. Light the scene with red candles. You might want to bake extra cake and cookies, so the centerpiece will stay intact for another celebration.

❄ Day one: bake cookies, make candy

Cut the cookies from Roll-out cookie dough (page 80) tinted flesh color. You'll need eight stars, eight boys, eight girls and Santa. As soon as stars are taken from the oven, place on a 6″ curved surface to cool. Cool rest of cookies flat.

Mold little lollipops in hard candy, page 80. When cool, wrap tightly in plastic wrap until ready to use.

❄ Day two: trim cookies, make cake

1. All the cookies are decorated in royal icing (page 80), using the flow-in method. Tint portions of the recipe in red, green and white and very small amounts in brown and yellow. Use tube 1 to outline color areas on all cookies. Now thin the icing with water so it flows easily from the cone with light pressure. Working from edges in, flow in the colors. Dry, then pipe all details with tube 1. For Santa, pipe beard, pompon and "fur" with tube 13. When dry, turn Santa and boy and girl cookies over and decorate the backs.

2. Bake a two-layer 6″ round cake. Chill, then set on 6″ cake circle and fill and ice with buttercream (page 43). Pipe a tube 20 shell border at base, reverse shell border at top. Pipe mounds of icing on backs of star cookies and press to cake sides.

3. Prepare two-part base as explained on page 6, using 1″ thick styrofoam for upper base. Lower base is 12″ round, upper base 10″. Ice upper base with royal icing then sprinkle with edible glitter. Attach to lower base with icing.

❄ Day three: put it all together

Secure cake to base with dabs of royal icing. Push a lollipop, straight up, in center of cake. Pipe a little mound of icing in front of it and set Santa in position, lollipop serving as prop. Arrange more lollipops around him.

Attach boy and girl cookies to upper base by piping dots of icing on back of each. At serving time, pass the cookies and lollipops and cut the cake into eight slices.

❄ Santa's landed!

This year he loaded his monoplane with surprises for children for the long flight from the North Pole. Reproduce the historic landing in gingerbread for an enchanting centerpiece. Colorful trim is cut from tinted Roll-out cookie dough. All recipes are on page 80.

Upper base is 14″ round, lower base 16″. Cover double cardboard with foil for lower base (see page 6). Ice double cardboard upper base with royal icing and sprinkle with edible glitter:

❄ Day one: bake cookie pieces.

Using patterns, cut out all gingerbread pieces from dough rolled less than ⅛″ thick. Using round cutters, cut 3″ and 1½″ wheels. Cut an extra 1½″ wheel for support for tail.

From tinted dough, cut star and circle trim, using miniature cutters. Tiny circles are cut with tubes 1A and 2A. Use cutter from Christmas set for Santa. Cut propeller by using pattern. Bake all pieces, then cool and crisp overnight.

❄ Day two: assemble plane, prepare details

1. Pipe lettering on side of plane with tube 1. Build body of plane as diagram shows, using royal icing as "glue". Assemble tail. Let body set about half an hour before putting on wing, tail and wheels. To make rear wheel assembly, cut a candy cane to 2½″ length. On one end, attach two 1½″ round cookies for wheels. On other end, attach another 1½″ round cookie in horizontal position to use as brace.

Attach all tinted cookie trim. With body of plane upside down, secure wheels and allow to set about an hour. Turn plane upright and attach tail and wing.

2. Pipe tree and bush as described on page 31. Pipe tube 3 ornaments on tree. Trim Santa cookie as shown on page 32. Prepare base. For gifts, wrap candy in thin foil and tie with gold string.

❄ Day three: put it all together

Cover seams on plane with tube 4 bulbs. Set plane, bush and tree on base, securing with a little icing. Pipe a mound of icing inside cockpit and place Santa in position, propping until set. Scatter the gifts on the snowy ground.

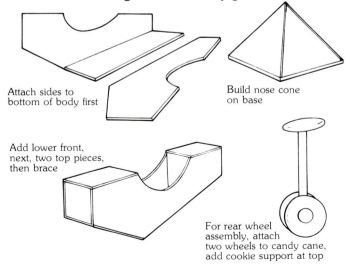

Attach sides to bottom of body first

Add lower front, next, two top pieces, then brace

Build nose cone on base

For rear wheel assembly, attach two wheels to candy cane, add cookie support at top

Santa loads his sleigh

Santa and his helpful elves are very busy on Christmas eve, loading his old-fashioned sleigh with gifts. Bright touches of marzipan decorate the sleigh.

This is an easy centerpiece to put together. Only the sleigh is cut from patterns—all other pieces are stamped out with cutters.

Upper base is a 12″ circle of 1″ thick styrofoam, lower base is 14″ in diameter.

❄ Day one: bake cookies, prepare base

You will need only about a third of the recipe for gingerbread on page 80—refrigerate rest for another purpose. Cut and bake pieces for sleigh. Use cutters from gingerbread set for elves, Christmas set for Santa. Lay cut-out Santa on two popsicle sticks for baking—ends of sticks projecting about 1″ from feet. Cool and crisp all cookies overnight.

Ice styrofoam upper base with royal icing and sprinkle with edible glitter. Attach to foil-covered lower base.

❄ Day two: make trims, assemble sleigh

For elves, outline suits with tube 1 and royal icing. Thin the icing with water and flow in areas. Pipe tube 4 shell-motion hats. Finish with tube 1 features and zig-zag trim. Use the same flow-in method for Santa's red suit. When dry, turn cookie over and repeat, covering popsicle sticks. Pipe tube 2 features, tube 13 beard and "fur" trim. Decorate back of cookie the same.

You will need only a tiny portion of marzipan (page 78) for trim. Tint, roll out and cut flowers and leaves with Flower Garden and Truffle cutters. Center flowers with circles, cut with tube 11. Dry trims about an hour then brush on hot glaze. When glaze is dry attach trims to sleigh pieces with dots of royal icing.

Assemble sleigh with royal icing. Lay bottom upside down and attach runners. When set, turn upright and secure one side to bottom, then front and back, propping until set. Add second side. Check seat for size and trim, if necessary. Pipe a line of icing on the inside of each side piece and set seat in position. Prop with crumpled foil.

❄ Day three: put it all together

Secure sleigh to base by piping a line of icing on bottoms of runners. Push popsicle sticks on Santa into base. Arrange elves on mounds of icing, then scatter gifts—these are candies wrapped in foil. Finish with a border of gumdrops.

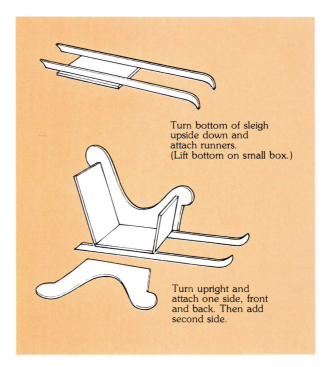

Turn bottom of sleigh upside down and attach runners. (Lift bottom on small box.)

Turn upright and attach one side, front and back. Then add second side.

Santa's sailing in!

He's bringing a boatload of toys and surprises for good little boys and girls! His good ship Ho-Ho is made of cake with a gingerbread deckhouse. The deckhouse is built on a 7″ square separator plate, so you can lift it off before serving the cake. Santa and his elves are cookies, too.

❄ Day one: bake cookies, prepare details

Cut Santa and several elves from Roll-out cookie dough (page 80), using Christmas and Gingerbread cutter sets. Cut deckhouse pieces from gingerbread. Bake all cookies, cool and crisp overnight.

❄ Day two: assemble deckhouse, bake cake

1. Decorate Santa and elves using the flow-in method, page 35. Assemble the deckhouse with royal icing on a 7″ square separator plate. Before putting on roof, attach elves to window openings on inside of house. Make ice cream cone tree (page 31) and paper or ribbon banner. Letter banner with tube 1s and attach to candy cane with icing.

2. Bake an 11″ x 15″ two-layer cake. Fill the layers, then chill for several hours. Trim off as diagram shows. Ice with buttercream, page 43, then set deckhouse in position. Stripe decorating cone with blue icing, fill with white icing and pipe tube 22 curved shells at base of boat. Pipe name with tube 2. Cover deckhouse seams with tube 14 shells. Pipe tube 233 wreaths, then add boiled icing snow and sprinkle with edible glitter.

3. Attach Santa and elves to deck on mounds of icing. We surrounded them with foil-wrapped candy and tiny toys. Trim about two dozen small candy canes to 3″ length. Pipe a tube 19 star border around top edge of cake, then push in candy canes. Drop tube 13 strings from "posts", then top with tube 8 upright shells. Set tree on roof, push in banner and add gum drop portholes. The SS Ho-Ho will serve 26.

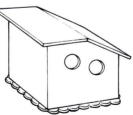

Build deckhouse on 7″ square separator plate. Roof is two-piece. Attach door last.

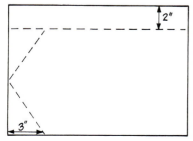

After filling two-layer 11″ x 15″ cake, trim to boat-shape as shown.

Santa's here!

Right on your holiday table! Would you believe this loveable elf is all cake and luscious buttercream icing? This diagram shows you just how he's put together.

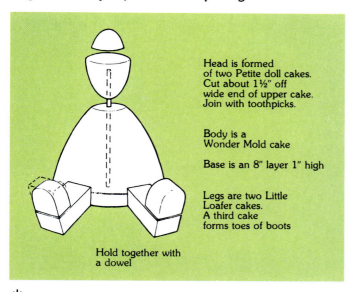

Head is formed of two Petite doll cakes. Cut about 1½" off wide end of upper cake. Join with toothpicks.

Body is a Wonder Mold cake

Base is an 8" layer 1" high

Legs are two Little Loafer cakes. A third cake forms toes of boots

Hold together with a dowel

❄ Prepare details, bake cake

1. Make the wreath by cutting out a 3½" cookie, then cutting a 2" hole in center to form a doughnut shape. Bake, then brush with thinned royal icing. When dry, turn over and brush other side. Pull out "needles" with tube 73, then pipe a tube 101 bow.

2. Tree starts with an ice cream cone. Cover with royal icing, and dry. Stuff with several marshmallows, then pipe more icing inside tree to fill crevices. Pipe trunk, about 1½" long, on wax paper with tube 10. When dry, insert trunk in tree and secure with icing. Cover tree with tube 73 needles.

3. For lower base, cover a double 14" cake circle with foil. (See page 6.) Attach a double 12" cake circle for upper base. Ice upper base with royal icing, sprinkle with edible glitter and border with tube 10 balls.

4. Bake cakes—an 8" x 1" layer, a Wonder Mold cake, three Little Loafers and two Petite doll cakes. Wrap tightly in plastic wrap and chill overnight. (Chilling makes cakes much easier to construct and decorate.)

❄ Assemble Santa

1. For legs, cut about 1" off two Little Loafer cakes and place on wax paper. From the third loaf cake, cut two pieces, each about 1½" long. Round off one end of each with a sharp knife for toes of boots. Attach these with buttercream to the other two pieces. Ice the legs, red on upper part, rest chocolate.

2. Stroke a little icing on an 8" cardboard cake circle and lay 1" layer on it. Ice top, then stack Wonder Mold cake. Insert a ¼" dowel, about 10" long, through both cakes, right down to cake circle. Push Petite doll cake over protruding dowel, ice top and add trimmed Petite doll

cake. Insert a few toothpicks, if necessary, to secure.

3. Ice the cake, red for body and hat, flesh color for lower head. Don't be concerned if edges are a little sloppy—trim will cover.

❄ Decorate Santa

1. Move the iced cake to the prepared base. Set legs against front of cake, securing with icing. Santa is beginning to take form!

2. Pipe features, using tube 8 for chubby cheeks, tube 5 for nose and eyes. Now figure pipe arms with tube 1A, starting at top rear of Wonder Mold cake and curving to front. Do not pipe hands at this time.
Pipe tube 19 zigzags for cuffs on pants, sleeves and hat. Use the same tube for swirls forming beard and hair, shells for mustache and fluffy pompon on hat.

3. Attach wreath over arm, securing with icing. Now lay tree over beard and shoulder, trimming tree at back as necessary. Figure pipe the mittens, curling over wreath and tree trunk. Finish Santa with tube 22 zigzags for fur hem of jacket and tube 9 buttons. Can you bear to cut him? Remove legs and head, wreath and tree. Cut main body of cake in half, vertically. Lay cut sides of halves down and slice each into seven generous slices. There'll be enough for 18 guests.

❄ Wilton Snow-white buttercream

A delicious, pure white icing that tints easily. For deep colors, tint to a slightly lighter tone than desired and let stand a few hours. Color will darken. Use this icing to cover the cake and for piping borders and other trims.

    ⅔ cup water
    4 tablespoons meringue powder
    1¼ cups solid white shortening, room temperature
    11½ cups confectioners' sugar, sifted
    ¾ teaspoon salt
    ¼ teaspoon butter flavoring
    ½ teaspoon almond flavoring
    ½ teaspoon clear vanilla flavoring

Combine water and meringue powder and whip at high speed until peaks form. Add four cups sugar, one cup at a time, beating after each addition at low speed. Alternately add shortening and remainder of sugar. Add salt and flavorings and beat at low speed until smooth. May be stored, well covered, in refrigerator for several weeks, then brought to room temperature and rebeaten. Yield: 8 cups. Recipe may be cut in half or doubled.

A wreath of poinsettias

The handsomest holiday centerpiece is a deluxe dessert, too. A rich fruitcake is crowned with scarlet marzipan poinsettias, then garnished with buttercream.

 ## In advance, bake the cake

You can do this even months ahead, then wrap the cake in a brandy-soaked towel, seal it in a plastic bag and set it aside in a cool place. The glorious flavors will ripen to perfection. This recipe is just the right size to bake in an 11″ ring pan. The shape is ideal for neat, even slices too.

BEST-EVER FRUITCAKE

    3 cups all-purpose flour
    2 teaspoons baking soda
    1 teaspoon baking powder
    ½ teaspoon cloves
    ½ teaspoon nutmeg
    ½ teaspoon cinnamon
    ½ teaspoon salt
    1 pound candied cherries
    ½ pound mixed candied fruit
    8-ounce jar candied pineapple
    ¾ cup dates
    1 cup raisins
    1½ cups chopped pecans (6-ounce package)
    1½ cups chopped walnuts (6-ounce package)
    ½ cup butter
    1 cup sugar
    2 eggs
    ½ cup white grape juice
    1½ cups applesauce (16-ounce can)

1. Preheat oven to 275°F. Sift and mix first seven ingredients. Cut up fruit and mix with nuts. Stir one cup of the sifted dry ingredients into fruit-nut mixture.

2. Cream butter and sugar. Add eggs and beat well. Beating until blended after each addition, alternately add remaining dry ingredients and grape juice to the creamed mixture. Mix in fruit-nut mixture and applesauce.

3. Turn into an 11″ ring pan that has been sprayed with non-stick pan release. Bake at 275° F. for two and a half hours. Run a knife around sides of pan and let cake set ten minutes in pan. Remove cake and cool thoroughly.

A day ahead, start marzipan trim

You will need one-third of the marzipan recipe (page 78). Tint one-fourth of it green and the rest red. Roll out green marzipan as recipe directs and cut out about 50 leaves with the holly leaf cutter. For red marzipan petals, cut out about 70 petals with the lily leaf cutter and about 30 petals with the small violet leaf cutter. (All cutters are from Flower Garden set.) Dust plastic curved surfaces with confectioners' sugar, and dry all marzipan pieces on and within curves.

The next day, assemble flowers. You will need eight to trim cake. Form a "doughnut" about 3″ in diameter from crumpled foil. Lay on wax paper. In the center, pipe a mound of royal icing with tube 9. Insert tips of petals into mound. Pipe another mound of icing in center of flower. Top with tube 4 yellow dots, then tube 3 red dots. Dry

thoroughly, at least several hours. Now brush leaves and flowers with Corn Syrup Glaze (page 78) and dry.

Put it all together

To glaze cake, heat one cup of apricot jam to boiling, strain and brush over surface while glaze is still hot. This glaze will seal the cake, keep it moist and add a tangy flavor. Place cake on serving tray and attach poinsettias with mounds of icing. Attach leaves. Pipe a tube 22 shell border with buttercream (page 43), place a candle in center of cake and start the party! Slice into 60 pieces, ½″ wide.

 # A spray of holly

Candy canes and holly leaves trim a centerpiece cake as merry as Christmas!

 ## In advance, make holly, bake cake

Make the holly leaves from marzipan, just as described for the poinsettia cake. You will need about 30 leaves—only about one sixth of the marzipan recipe on page 78. Cut a 2″ x 1½″ gift tag from rolled marzipan and pipe greeting with tube 1s.

Bake the two-layer cake in 12″ petal-shaped pans, making sure each layer is about 2″ high. Wrap layers tightly in plastic wrap and refrigerate overnight.

Decorate the cake

Fill and ice the cake smoothly with buttercream (page 43). Pipe a tube 19 shell border at top and bottom. Near base of cake, pipe two swirls on each curve with tube 22. Use tube 19 to pipe fleurs-de-lis above swirls, then add stars with same tube. On top of cake, pipe tube 22 swirls and trim with tube 19 shells and stars.

Wire three candy canes together with florists' wire and place on top of cake. Arrange holly leaves and gift card around candy canes. Make a small arrangement of miniature candy canes and holly on side of cake, attaching with icing. Attach red ribbon bows with dots of icing. Serve to 24, cutting three slices from each curve of the cake.

A Christmas merry-go-round

Candy canes, prancing horses and a colorful cookie canopy makes this the merriest Christmas cake! It's quick to put together, using the Carousel separator set.

❋ Do details in advance

1. Using patterns, cut eight-piece canopy from tinted Roll-out cookie dough (page 80). Bake and set aside.

2. Using royal icing (page 80) and tube 233, pipe wreaths on horses. Add tube 101s bows.

3. Mold two hollow sugar molds (page 80) in Petite doll pan for tree and support for canopy. Decorate tree with royal icing as shown on page 31. Add tube 4 balls. Make a banner of ribbon or colored paper, glue to a toothpick and do lettering with tube 1s.

4. Build canopy using royal icing as glue. Set up Carousel separator set, attaching tree in center of lower plate with icing. Attach un-iced sugar mold to center of upper plate. Pipe a line of icing on base of one canopy section and set on upper plate—point resting on sugar mold support. Pipe icing on one side and base of second section and set in position against first section. Continue until all sections are attached. Embossed cross on separator plate will guide you in placing the sections.

❋ Decorate the cake

1. Bake a two-layer cake in 12″ round pans. Make sure each layer is 2″ high. Fill and ice with buttercream (page 43), then set on serving tray. Insert a circle of ½″ dowels in cake, then clip off level with top of cake. This will support weight of Carousel. Center the separator set on cake. Trim eight candy canes to height of cake.

2. On top edge of cake, make eight evenly spaced marks, using posts on separator set as guide. Pipe a base border of tube 19 rosettes. Drop tube 19 string guidelines from mark to mark from top edge of cake, then pipe a reverse shell top border with same tube. Edge separator plate with tube 16 shells.
Pipe tube 233 garlands over string guidelines, then press candy canes into cake sides.

3. Trim canopy. Pipe tube 16 shells over seams. Use the same tube to pipe zigzag garlands at base. Pipe eight shells at peak of canopy, then insert banner.

4. Finish the trim by piping tube 65 ruffled leaves and tube 3 berries on edge of canopy. Attach red ribbon bows above candy canes with dots of icing. Serve this merry cake to 22—the cookie canopy a bonus for nibbling.

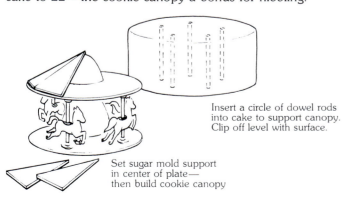

Insert a circle of dowel rods into cake to support canopy. Clip off level with surface.

Set sugar mold support in center of plate— then build cookie canopy

A cottage made of cake!

Just as charming as a gingerbread house, but this little cottage is made of cake! Bake it in a two-piece house-shaped pan, using two cake mixes. We trimmed this cottage with molded candies for a Christmas-y effect, but you'll dream up unique trims of your own.

❋ Prepare base and mold candies

1. For lower base, cover double 12″ cake circles with foil. For upper base, ice double 10″ cake circles with royal icing. Sprinkle with edible glitter and attach to lower base.

2. Mold confectionery coating candies using method described on page 24. You will need about 40 small hearts, about 20 small Christmas trees, eight squares for chimney and shutters, and several tree-shaped lollipops. Mold about 100 discs for roofing. Cut square candies in half, and trim sticks on lollipops to ½″.

❋ Bake and decorate cake

1. Use mixes or your favorite recipe to bake the cake in the two-piece house pan. Each half-pan will take one cake mix. Chill the baked cake for several hours, then assemble the two halves with buttercream (page 43) on a 6½″ square of corrugated cardboard. Level ridge of roof with a sharp knife, if necessary. Ice with buttercream.

2. Pipe lines of icing for door with tube 48, then outline with tube 2. Pipe window frames with tube 1. Attach half-square candies for shutters and heart candies for side windows. Outline eaves with tube 2B, then edge with tube 4 beading. Pull out needles on wreaths with tube 1 and add bow and berries with same tube. Pipe leaf trim on heart windows and at point of eaves with tube 349. Add tube 2 berries.

3. Transfer house to prepared base, first stroking a little icing on base to secure. Attach two candy half-squares for chimney. Starting at bottom, cover roof with rows of candy shingles. Pipe a dot of icing on back of disc, then press to roof. Pipe a line of icing on ridge of roof and press in purchased candy. Surround foundation of house with candies.

4. Landscape yard. Attach a candy square for doorstep. Make a candy path and edge with half-discs. Make holes in base with tip of sharp knife and insert sticks on lollipop trees. Add smaller candy trees. Finish with a border of upright candy hearts, piping a dot of buttercream on back of each to secure.

To serve your little cottage, cut vertically in half, through ridge of roof. Lay halves cut-side down and slice each into 12 servings for a total of 24.

Celebrate the new year!

We brought back this *Celebrate! Annual* star to charm your guests with a creation that's dessert and centerpiece all in one! This quaint cuckoo clock is constructed of cake and gingerbread with delicious marzipan trim and a fillip of miniature pretzels.

❋ **Day one: prepare marzipan, gingerbread, cake**

Using patterns, cut and bake gingerbread roof and gable pieces. Mark roof pieces for scallops. Cool and crisp overnight.

Make a recipe of marzipan and reserve half for another purpose. Tint brown, red and green and a tiny portion yellow. Leave a small amount untinted. Roll out about ⅛″ thick and cut bird house and clock face from patterns, leaves with small ivy leaf cutter, flowers with forget-me-not cutter. (Use Flower Garden cutter set.) Dry leaves within curved form, other pieces flat. Join double bird house and clock face pieces with egg white. Hand-model the cuckoo, shown here actual size, and pipe beak and eyes with tube 1. Glaze marzipan pieces. Pipe clock numbers and beading with tube 2. Using pattern, make a paper flag, letter with tube 1 and glue to a toothpick.

Bake three 8″ square layers, using your favorite cake recipe. Fill to achieve a height of 6″. Wrap tightly in plastic wrap and chill overnight.

❋ **Day two: decorate the clock**

Ice cake with buttercream icing. Using chocolate icing, outline each side with tube 1D. Pull up a tube 20 shell from each corner, then add tube 2 beading. Pipe a tube 1D line at top edges of two gingerbread gable pieces. Pipe tube 2 curving stems on all four sides of cake.

Mound icing on cake top at front and back and set gables in position. Do the same on other two sides and carefully place roof sections on gables. Pipe a line of icing on ridge of roof. Hold for a moment to set. Pipe zigzag scallops on roof with tube 2. Attach marzipan birdhouse, clock face, ivy leaf and flower trim to clock with icing. Ice heart-shaped "door" to a toothpick and attach in open position. Insert a

toothpick for cuckoo's perch and attach bird. Finish by securing pretzels to roof with icing and inserting flagpole. Just as cute as it can be! Serves 16, with gingerbread a bonus for nibbling.

Would you like a larger cake to serve a crowd? Set the cuckoo clock on a 12″ or larger square cake.

❋ **Cheerful cookie wreaths** page 1

Make several of these delicious decorations to hang on the wall, serve as a centerpiece with a fat candle in the center, or give to special friends. These wreaths are truly quick and easy to create—and they're ideal for using up leftover gingerbread and cookie dough. A fourth-recipe of Roll-out cookies and one-fourth of the gingerbread recipe (page 80) will be enough for three or four wreaths.

1. For each wreath, roll out gingerbread to about ⅛″ thickness on the back of a lightly greased cookie sheet (page 6). Cut out the ring-shaped base, following pattern, then cut out eight gingerbread hearts with a 2⅜″ cutter. Remove scraps from sheet. For a hanging wreath, cut a 2″ length of cloth-covered florists' wire, twist into a loop and press into the ring base at one of the outer notches. Brush base with cool water, then lay the cut-out hearts on it, matching indentation of each heart to a notch on base. Set aside.

2. Divide a fourth-recipe of Roll-out cookies into halves. Take a small portion from one half and tint yellow. Tint remainder of half-portion bright green. Tint second half-portion red. Wrap tinted dough in plastic until ready to roll out.

3. Preheat oven to 325°F. Roll out red-tinted dough on lightly floured surface and cut out eight hearts with a 1⅝″ cutter. Brush backs of hearts with water, then place on wreath as picture shows. Roll out green dough, cut out eight hearts with a 1″ cutter, brush backs with water and place on gingerbread hearts. Finally, roll out yellow dough and cut 16 circles with tube 2A. Place on gingerbread and red hearts, first brushing backs with water. Bake wreath about 13 minutes, until cookies are firm but not browned. Remove to cake rack with a large spatula to cool. Repeat for additional wreaths.

Roof--cut 2

 Celebrate! Christmas patterns

You'll find all the full-size patterns you need for projects in this book on the pages that follow.

To use the patterns, first trace as accurately as possible on parchment paper (wax paper is too flimsy). Then true up any straight lines with a ruler. Cut out the patterns and lightly spray with non-stick pan release. Now they are ready to lay on the rolled-out cookie dough and cut around with a very sharp knife. An artist's x-acto knife with a number 11 blade is a perfect tool.

As you cut out the cookie pieces, keep this book open to the pages on which the patterns are printed. Check carefully to be sure you are cutting the correct number of pieces from each pattern.

For more durable patterns that are easier to use, transfer your tracings to light cardboard, using carbon paper. Then cut out and spray with non-stick pan release.

Keep your patterns in a large envelope, carefully labeled. You'll be able to use them many times for future architectural projects.

❄ Index of patterns

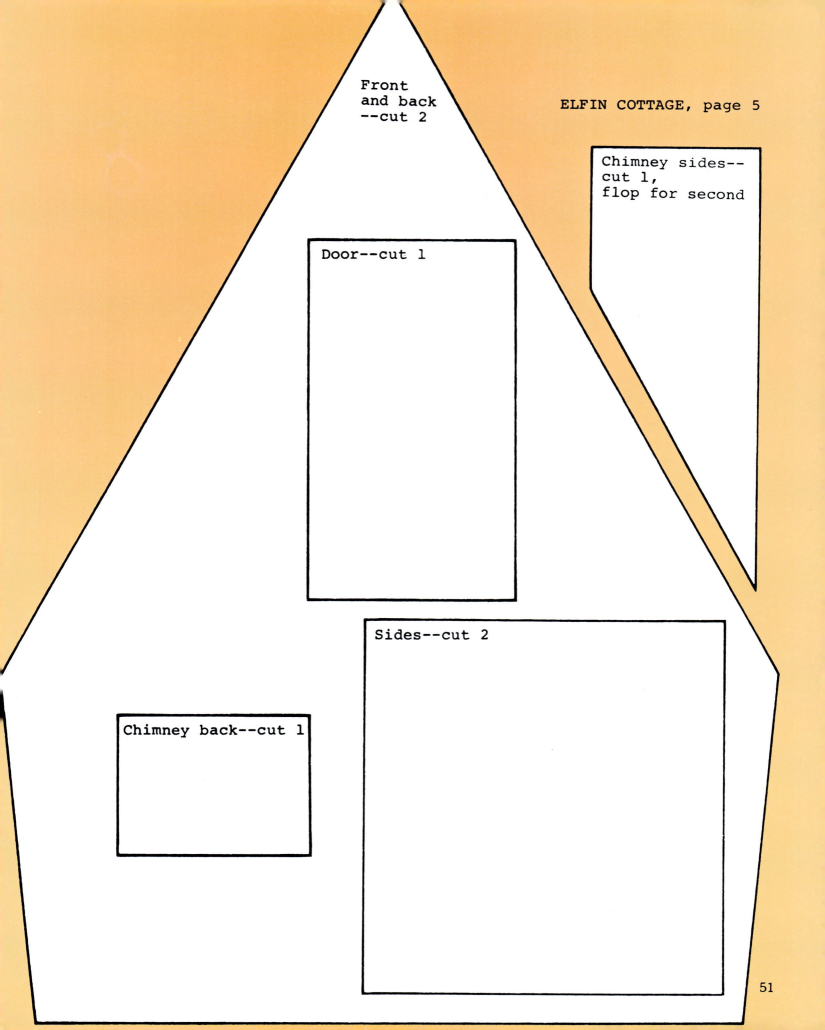

Front
and back
--cut 2

Chimney sides--
cut 1,
flop for second

Door--cut 1

Sides--cut 2

Chimney back--cut 1

51

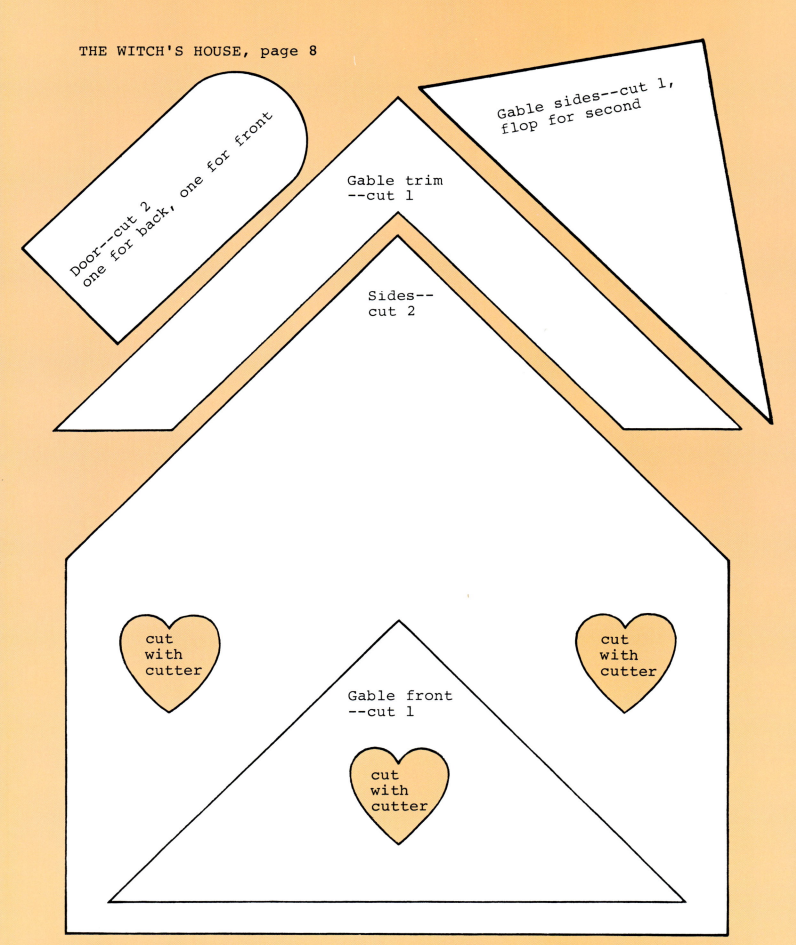

Door--cut 2
one for back, one for front

Gable sides--cut 1,
flop for second

Gable trim
--cut 1

Sides--
cut 2

cut
with
cutter

cut
with
cutter

Gable front
--cut 1

cut
with
cutter

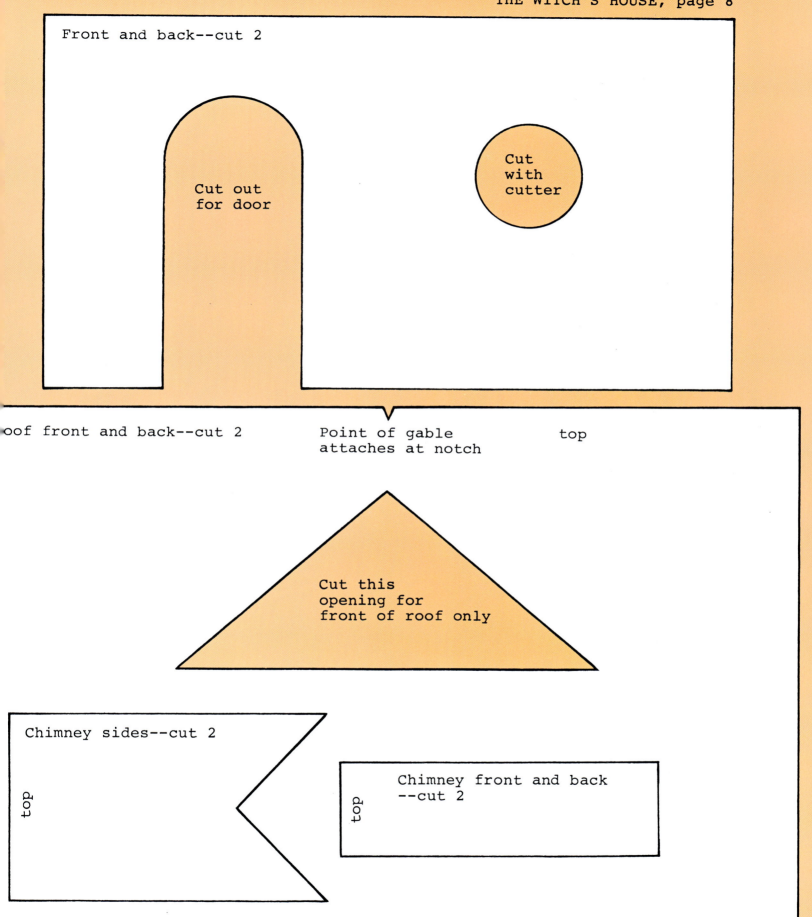

Front and back--cut 2

Cut out
for door

Cut
with
cutter

oof front and back--cut 2

Point of gable
attaches at notch

top

Cut this
opening for
front of roof only

Chimney sides--cut 2

top

Chimney front and back
--cut 2

top

Braces for
Mary and
Joseph
--cut 4

Sides--cut one,
flop for second

top

Cut
hearts
with
cutter

Brace
for
roof--
cut 2

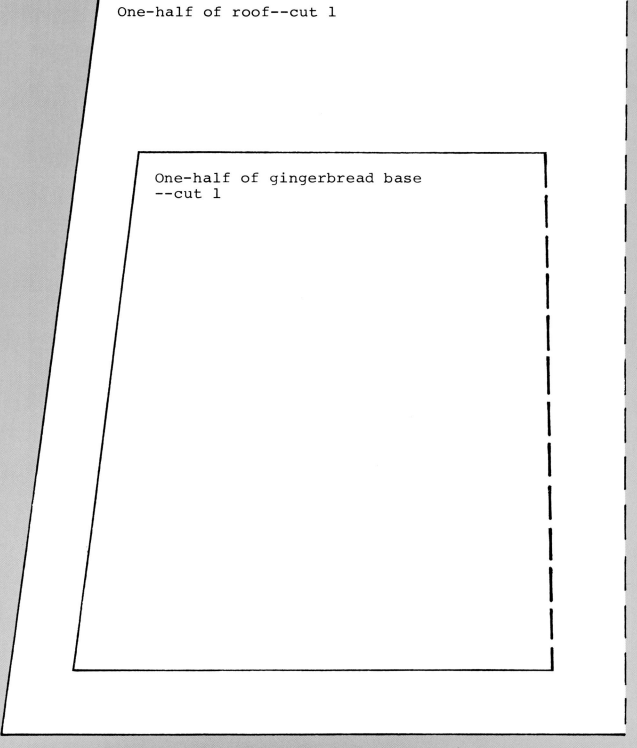

One-half of roof--cut 1

One-half of gingerbread base
--cut 1

Continued on next page

Back--cut 1

top

cut with cutter

Manger--
cut 1

Manger brace
cut 1

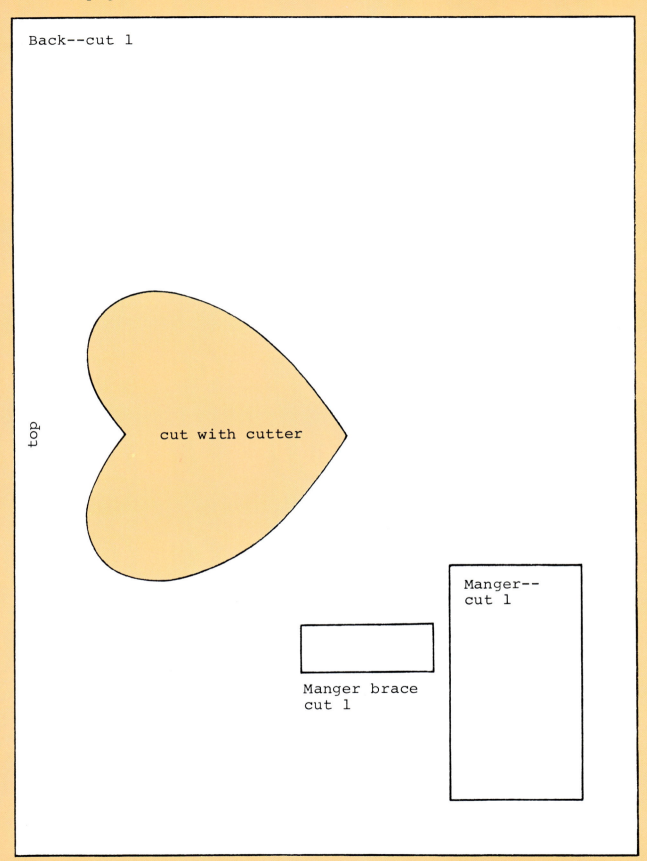

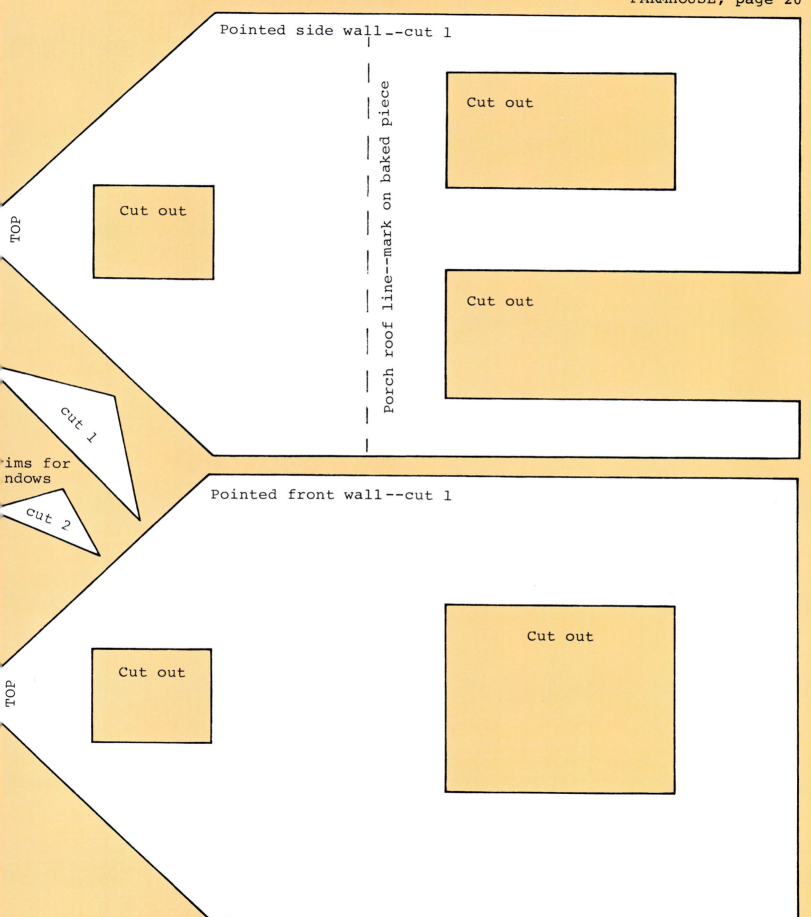

Pointed side wall--cut 1

Cut out

Cut out

TOP

Porch roof line--mark on baked piece

Cut out

cut 1

rims for
ndows

cut 2

Pointed front wall--cut 1

TOP

Cut out

Cut out

Cut out

Continued on next page

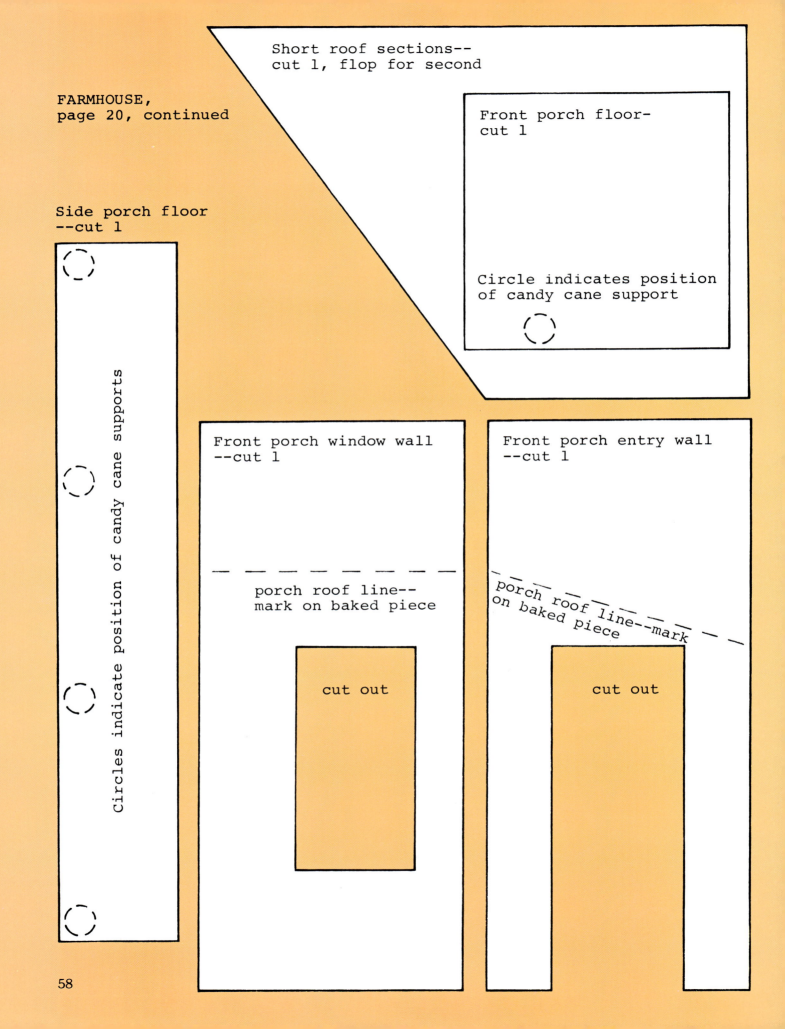

Short roof sections--
cut 1, flop for second

Side porch floor
--cut 1

Front porch floor-
cut 1

Circle indicates position
of candy cane support

Circles indicate position of candy cane supports

Front porch window wall
--cut 1

Front porch entry wall
--cut 1

porch roof line--
mark on baked piece

porch roof line--mark
on baked piece

cut out

cut out

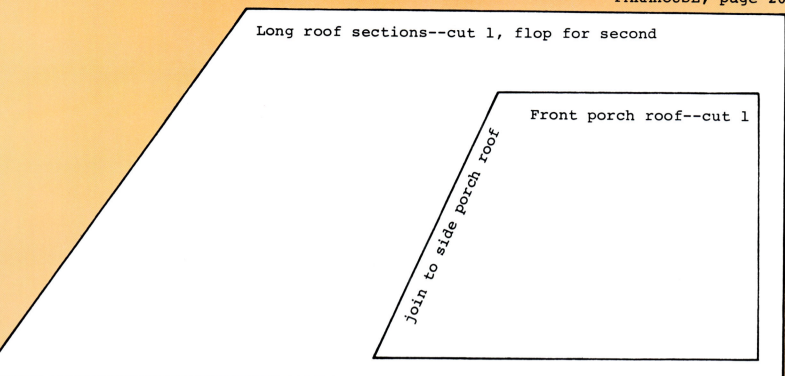

Long roof sections--cut 1, flop for second

Front porch roof--cut 1

join to side porch roof

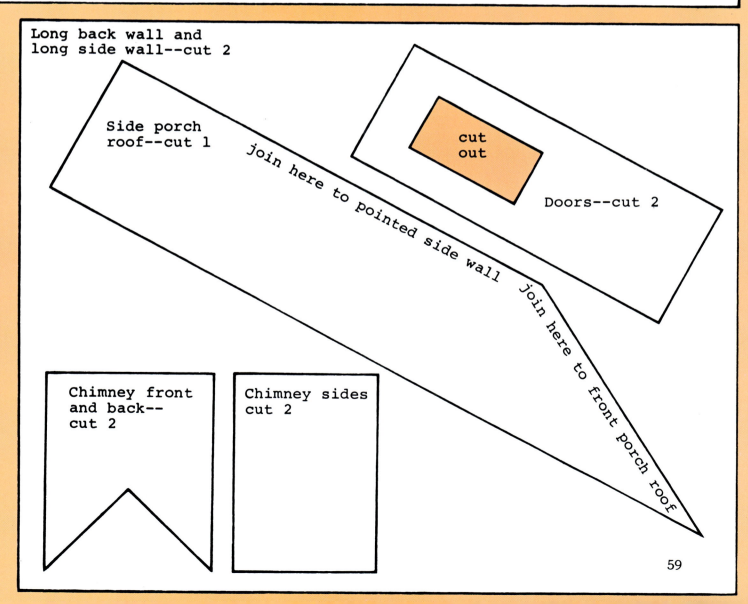

Long back wall and
long side wall--cut 2

Side porch
roof--cut 1

join here to pointed side wall

cut
out

Doors--cut 2

join here to front porch roof

Chimney front
and back--
cut 2

Chimney sides
cut 2

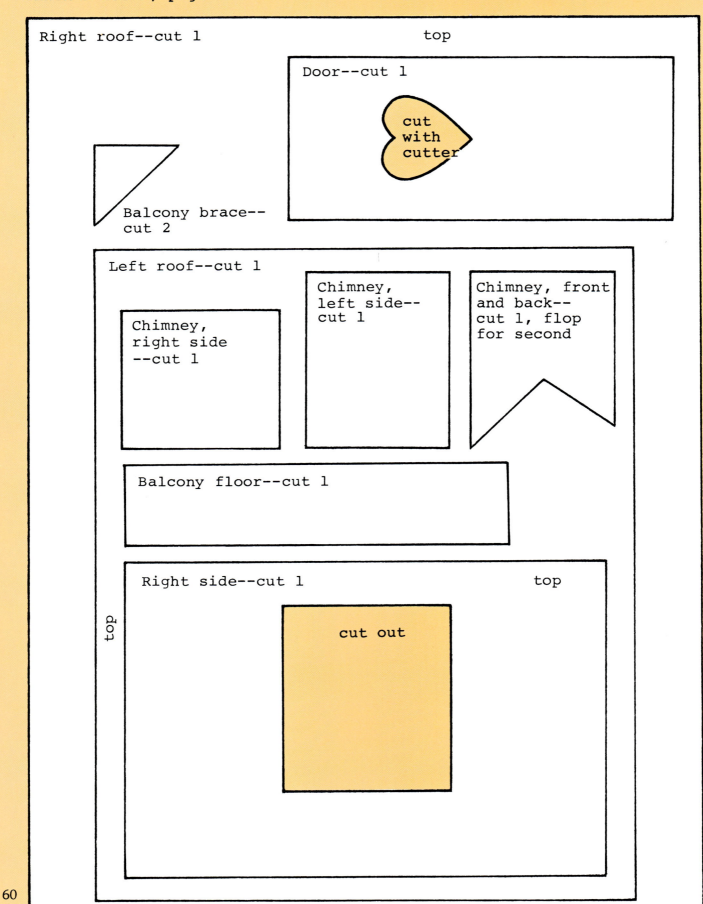

Right roof--cut 1   top

Door--cut 1

cut
with
cutter

Balcony brace--
cut 2

Left roof--cut 1

Chimney,
left side--
cut 1

Chimney, front
and back--
cut 1, flop
for second

Chimney,
right side
--cut 1

Balcony floor--cut 1

Right side--cut 1   top

top

cut out

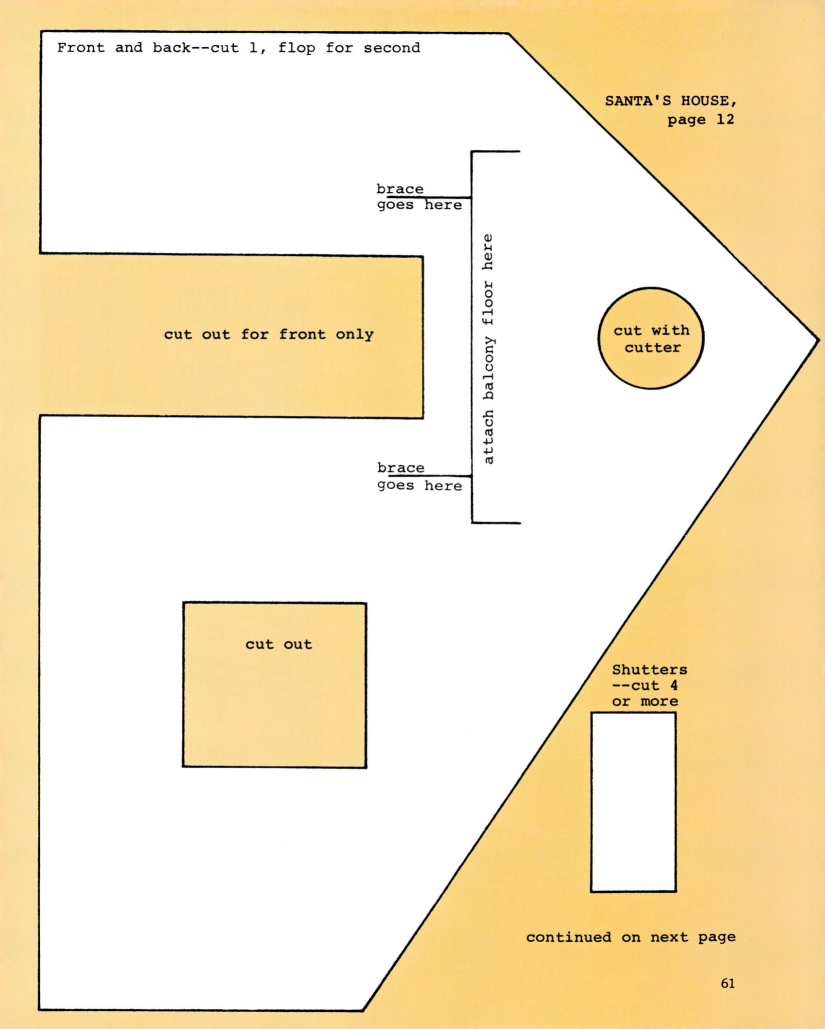

Front and back--cut 1, flop for second

brace
goes here

attach balcony floor here

cut with
cutter

cut out for front only

brace
goes here

cut out

Shutters
--cut 4
or more

continued on next page

SANTA'S HOUSE, page 12, continued
and VICTORIAN BROWNSTONE, page 17

Santa's house, left side--cut 1 top

cut out

VICTORIAN BROWNSTONE
stairway.
Cut in one strip
from ¼" thick
gingerbread

Bottom step--
join pattern to
step 2 (right)
to make
one strip

Top step

Step 6

Step 5

Step 4

Step 3

Step 2

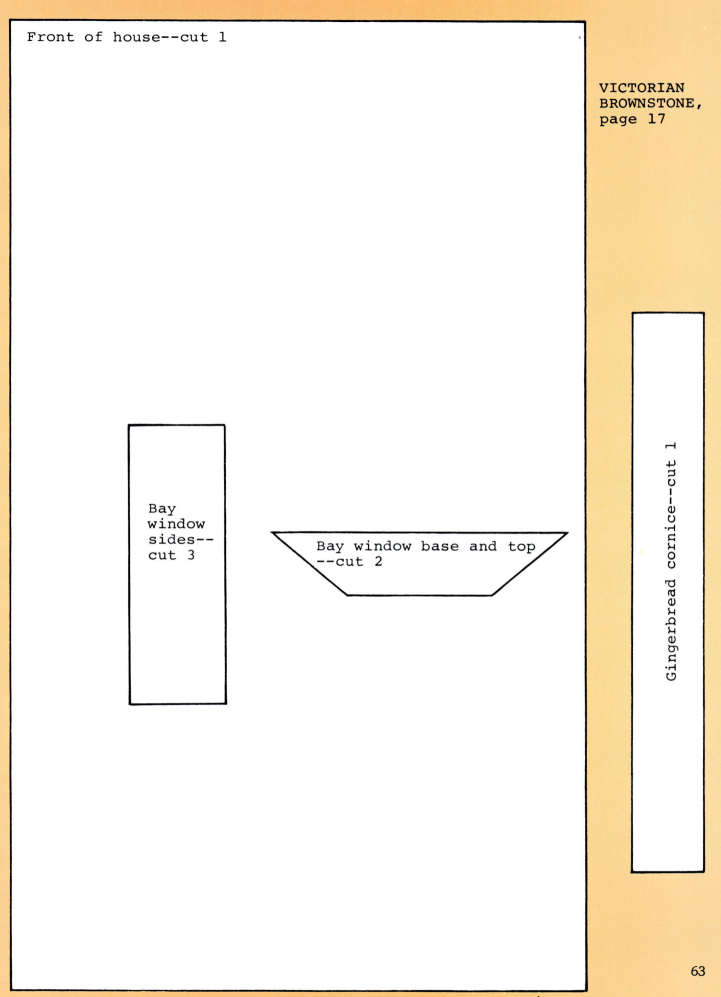

Front of house--cut 1

Bay window sides-- cut 3

Bay window base and top --cut 2

Gingerbread cornice--cut 1

continued on next page

One-half of back--
add windows as desired

One-half of roof

Sides of house--
cut 1, flop for second

All pieces below are cut from marzipan

Bay window
center roof
and center
support--
cut 2

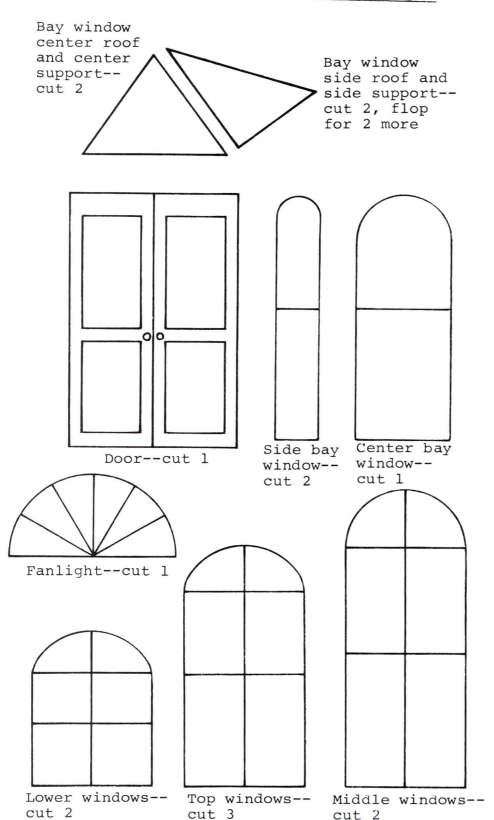

Bay window
side roof and
side support--
cut 2, flop
for 2 more

Marzipan cornice--
cut with same
pattern as
gingerbread cornice.
Cut curves with
base of
standard tube

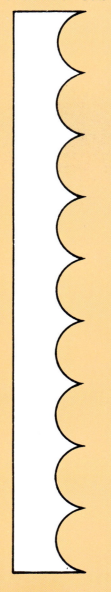

Door--cut 1

Side bay
window--
cut 2

Center bay
window--
cut 1

Fanlight--cut 1

Lower windows--
cut 2

Top windows--
cut 3

Middle windows--
cut 2

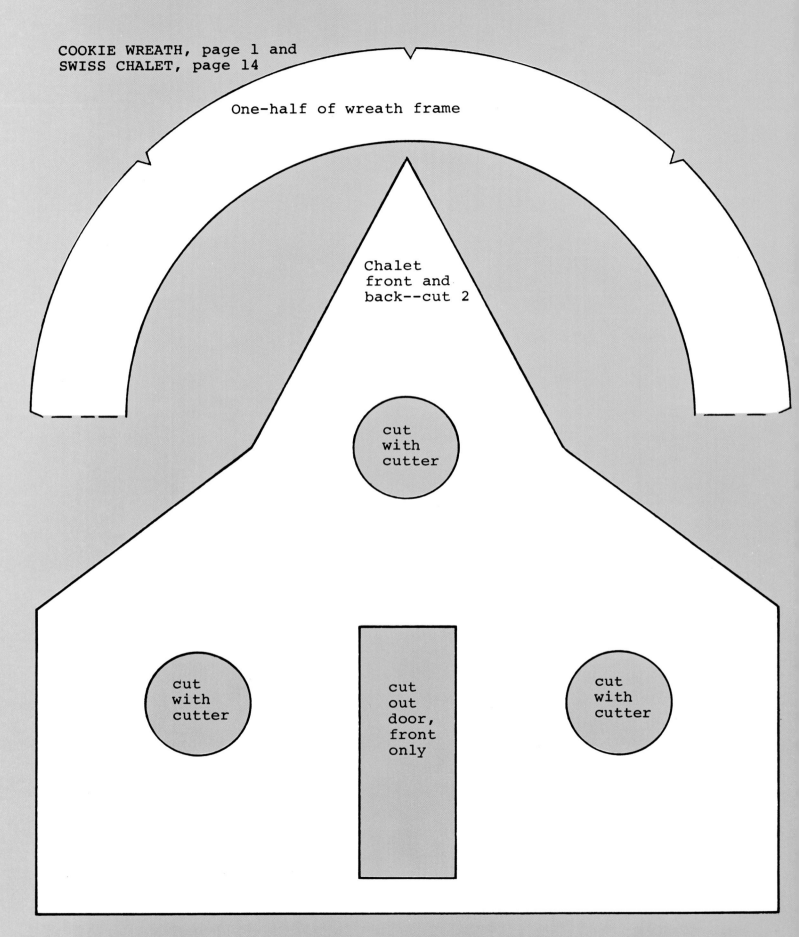

COOKIE WREATH, page 1 and
SWISS CHALET, page 14

One-half of wreath frame

Chalet
front and
back--cut 2

cut
with
cutter

cut
with
cutter

cut
out
door,
front
only

cut
with
cutter

Lower door step--
cut 1

Upper
door step--
cut 1

Door--cut 1

Upper roof--cut 2

Chimney front and back--
cut 2

top

Chimney sides--cut 2

top

Lower roof--cut 2

Sides--cut 2

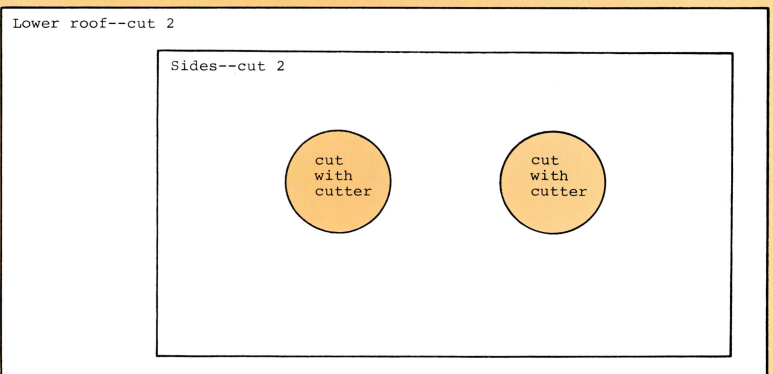

cut
with
cutter

cut
with
cutter

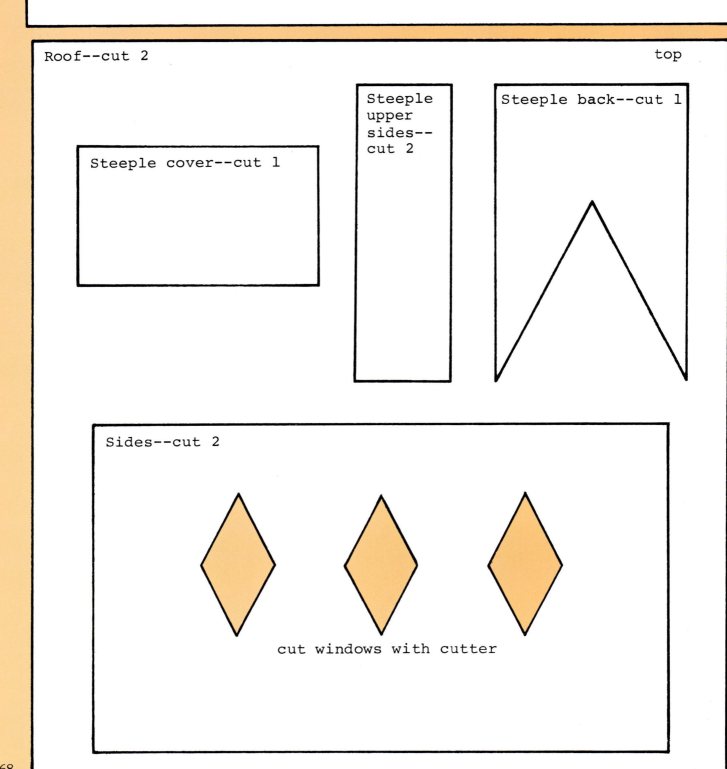

Steeple lower sides--cut 2

Roof--cut 2   top

Steeple cover--cut 1

Steeple upper sides-- cut 2

Steeple back--cut 1

Sides--cut 2

cut windows with cutter

Steeple front--
cut 1

Steeple roof,
front and back
--cut 2

Door--
cut 1

Steeple
roof
sides
--cut 2

Front and back--cut 2

cut
with
cutter

cut out
rectangle
for front
only

cut with
cutter

cut with
cutter

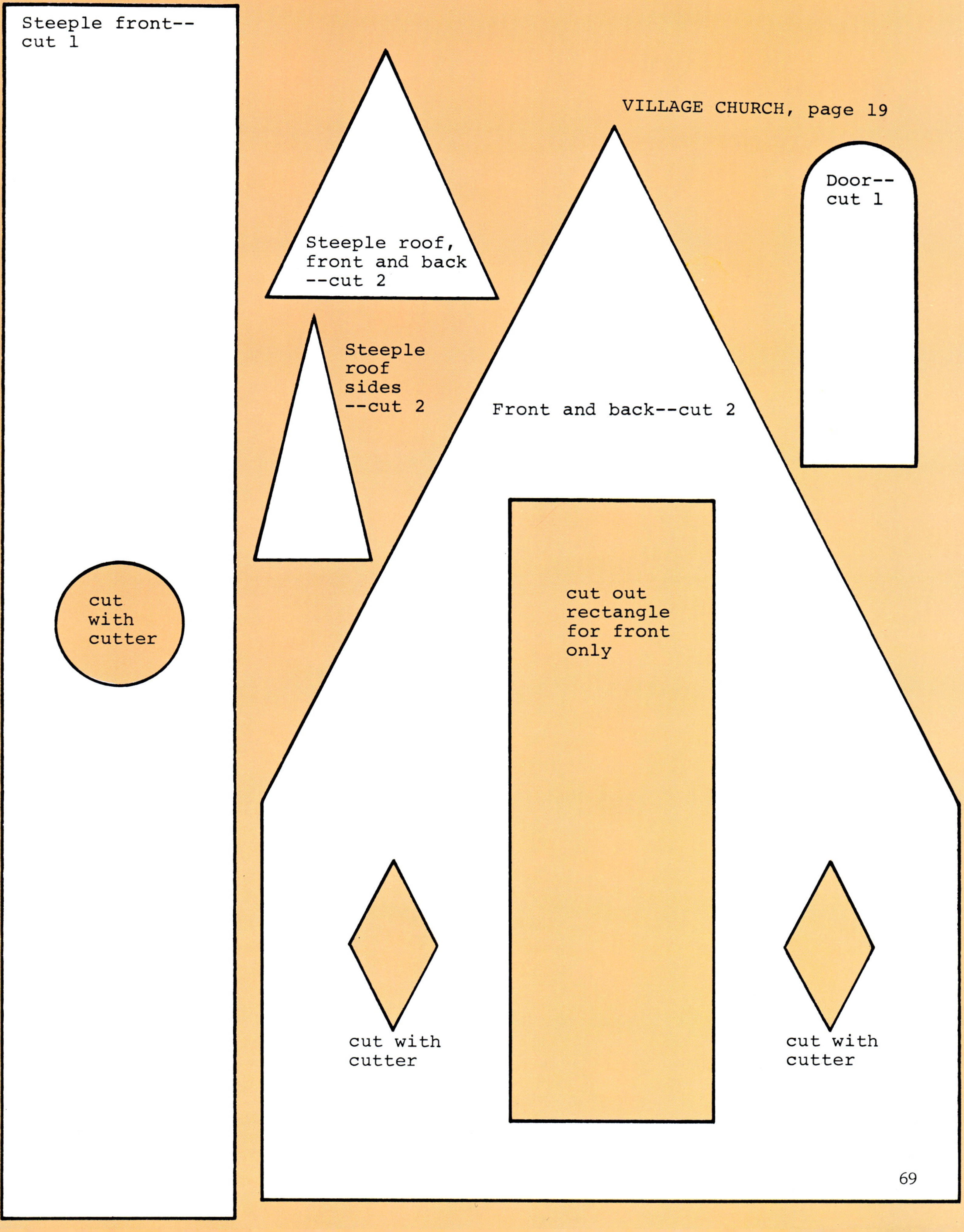

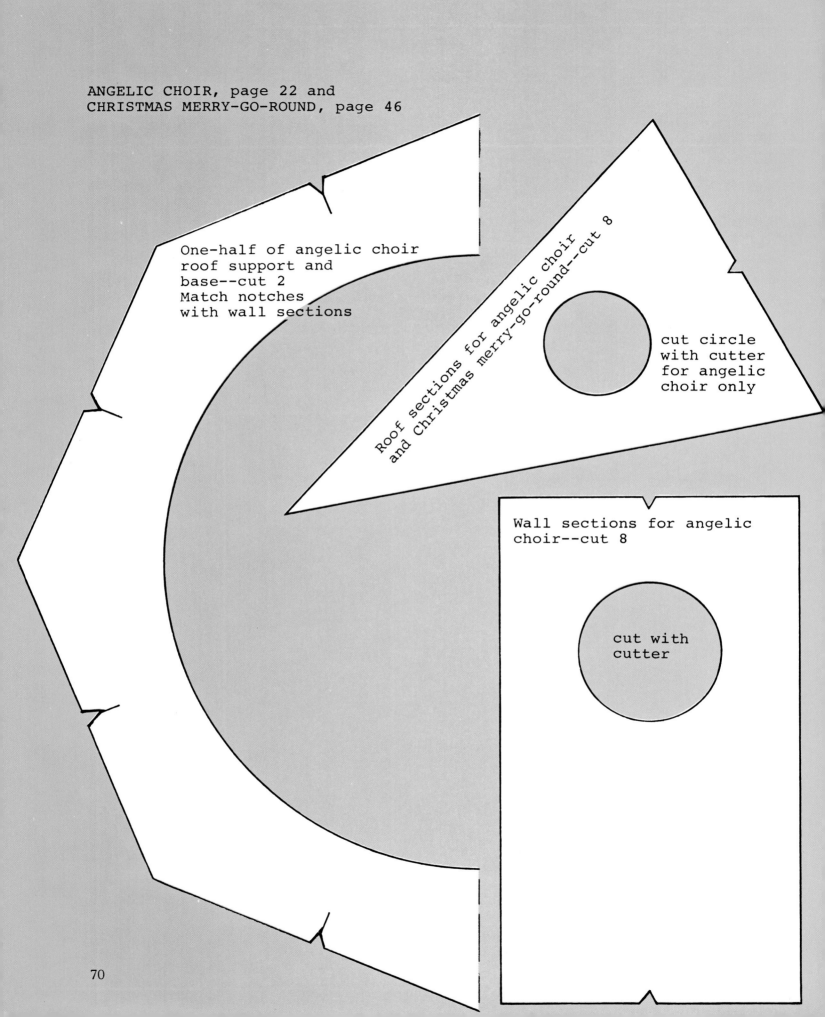

One-half of angelic choir
roof support and
base--cut 2
Match notches
with wall sections

Roof sections for angelic choir
and Christmas merry-go-round--cut 8

cut circle
with cutter
for angelic
choir only

Wall sections for angelic
choir--cut 8

cut with
cutter

70

Lid--cut 2

cut with cutter

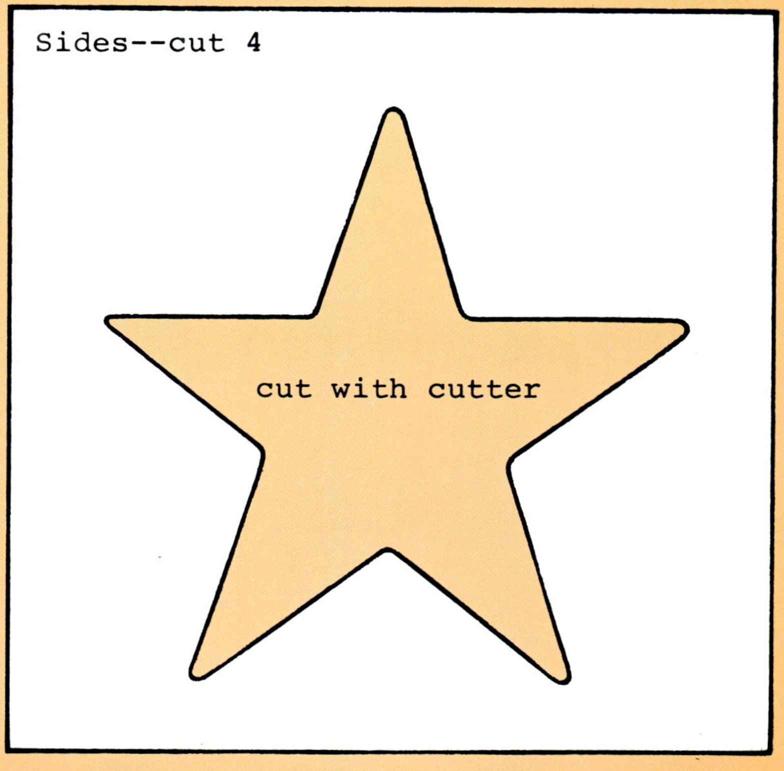

Sides--cut 4

cut with cutter

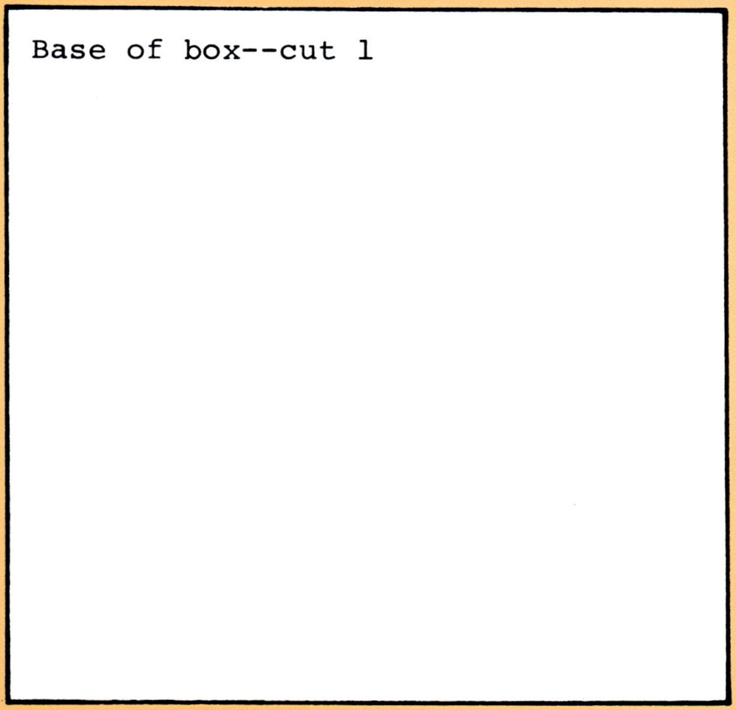

Base of box--cut 1

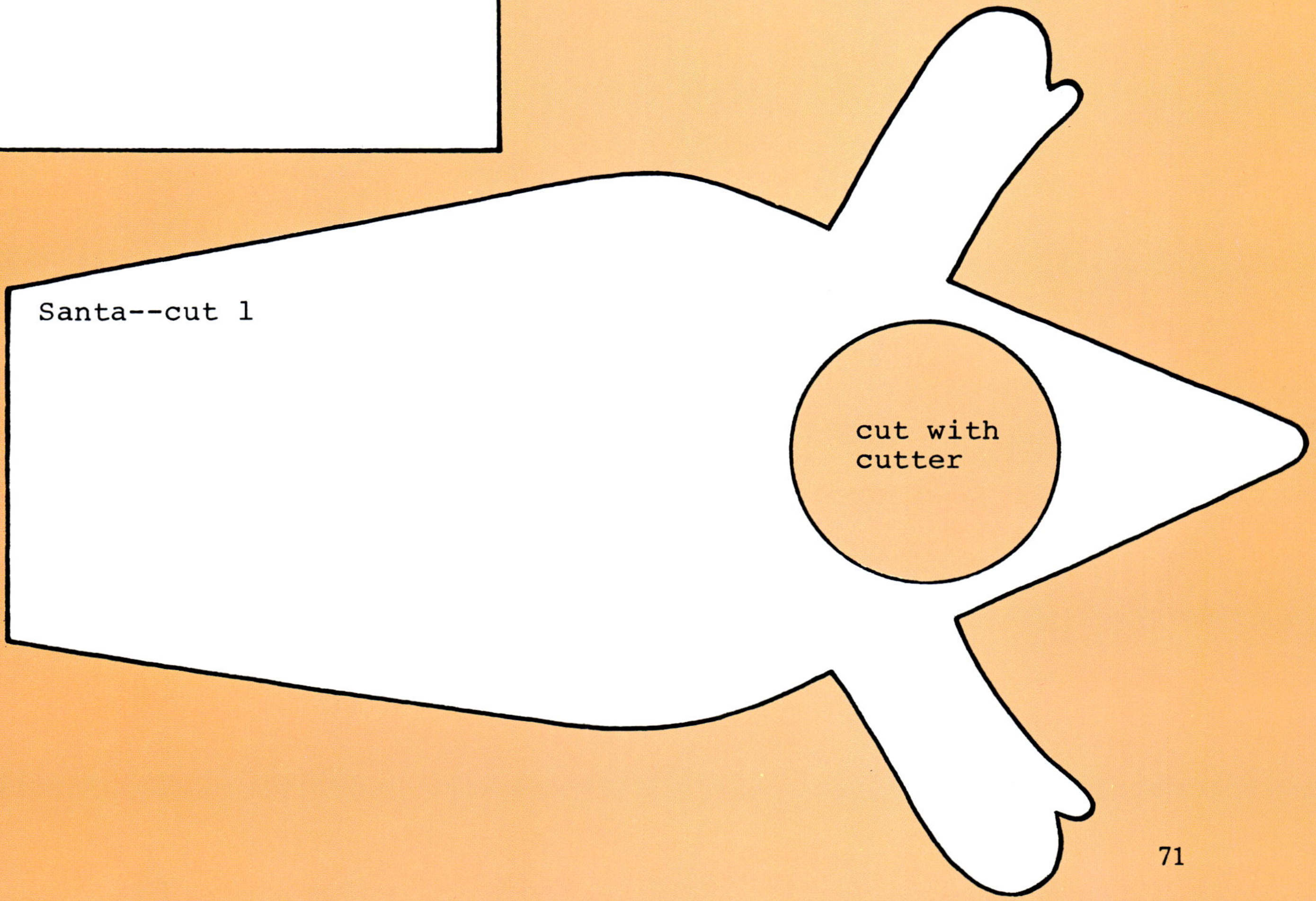

Santa--cut 1

cut with cutter

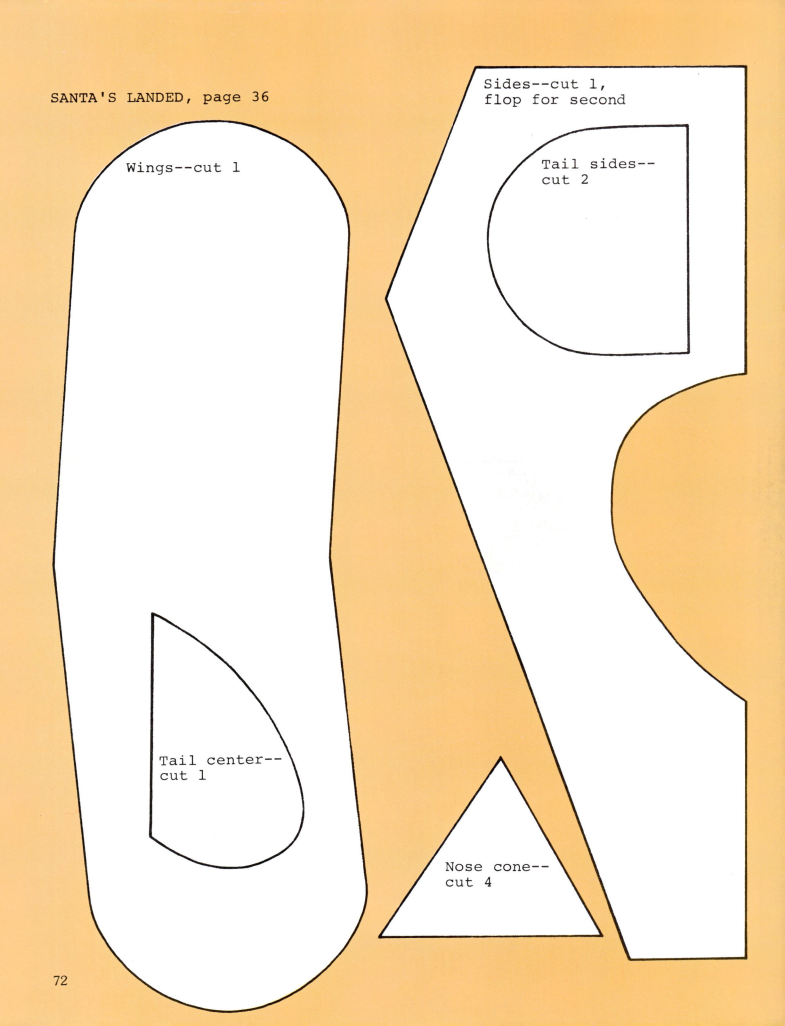

Wings--cut 1

Sides--cut 1,
flop for second

Tail sides--
cut 2

Tail center--
cut 1

Nose cone--
cut 4

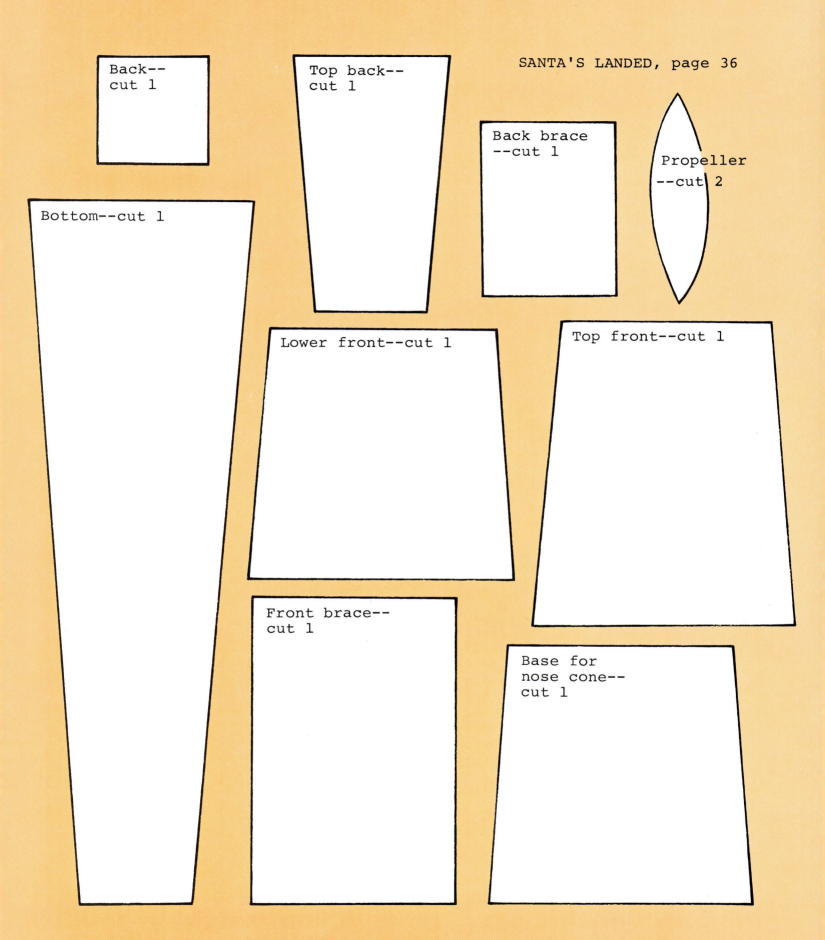

Back--
cut 1

Top back--
cut 1

Back brace
--cut 1

Propeller
--cut 2

Bottom--cut 1

Lower front--cut 1

Top front--cut 1

Front brace--
cut 1

Base for
nose cone--
cut 1

Deckhouse front roof--cut 1

Deckhouse sides--
cut 1, flop for second

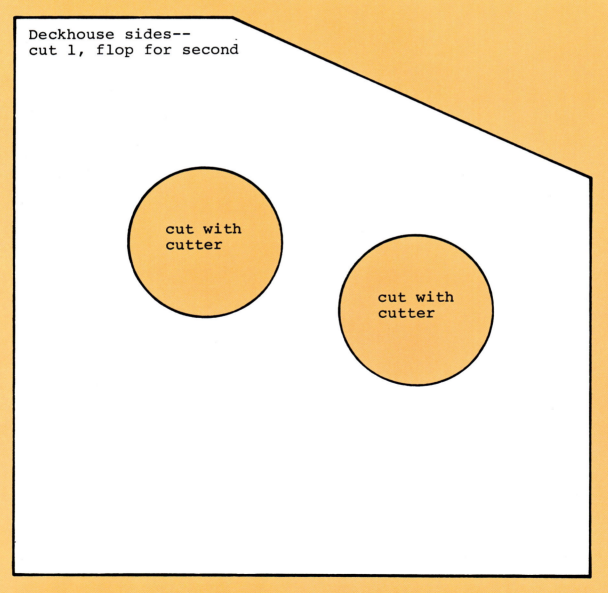

cut with
cutter

cut with
cutter

SS HO HO

Lettering on side of ship

One-half of deckhouse front--cut 1

Deckhouse rear roof--cut 1

Deckhouse back--cut 1   top

Deckhouse door--cut 1

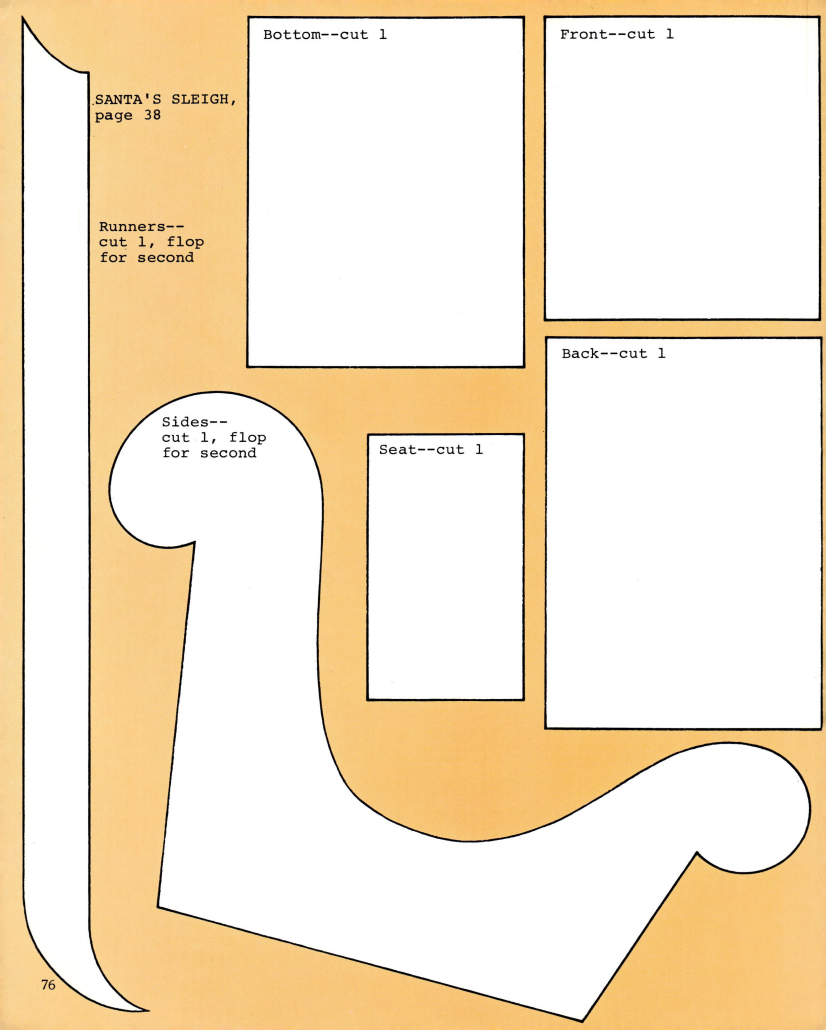

SANTA'S SLEIGH,
page 38

Runners--
cut 1, flop
for second

Sides--
cut 1, flop
for second

Bottom--cut 1

Front--cut 1

Back--cut 1

Seat--cut 1

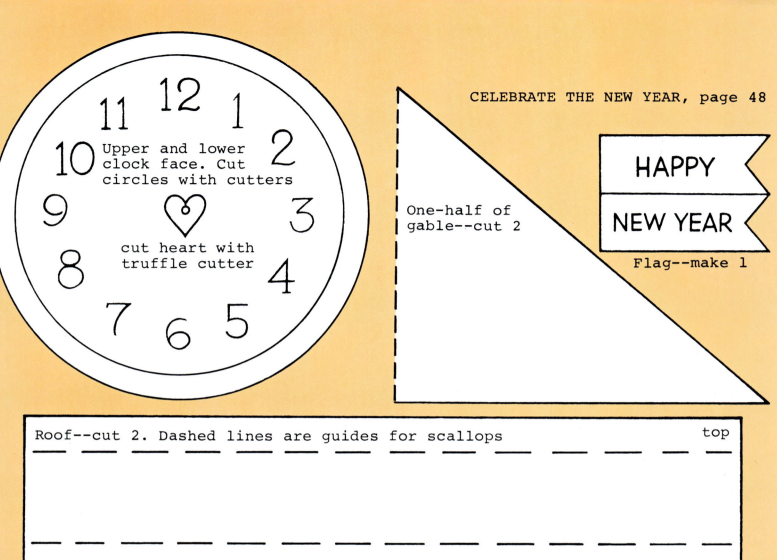

Upper and lower clock face. Cut circles with cutters

cut heart with truffle cutter

One-half of gable--cut 2

HAPPY

NEW YEAR

Flag--make 1

Roof--cut 2. Dashed lines are guides for scallops   top

Upper and lower birdhouse

cut with cutter

77

Marzipan...the magic mixture

Master the simple arts of marzipan and you'll hold the key to all kinds of pretty trims and confections! Marzipan is easy to put together, tastes delicious, tints easily and, well wrapped, keeps for months in the refrigerator.

Roll out marzipan like pie dough and cut all kinds of fancy shapes with cutters or a sharp knife. Or model marzipan into charming fairy tale figures. You'll be amazed at your skill as a sculptor!

❄ Wilton basic marzipan

An easy, all-purpose recipe for modelling figures or for rolled cut-out trims.

    8 ounces almond paste
    2 egg whites, unbeaten
    ½ teaspoon vanilla or rum flavoring
    3½ cups sifted confectioners' sugar (approximate)

1. Crumble almond paste in a large mixing bowl. Add egg whites and flavoring and knead until thoroughly mixed. Now add the sugar, a cup at a time, and knead very thoroughly after each addition until no lumps remain. Add enough sugar to the mixture so that marzipan has the texture of heavy pie dough. The entire process will take about 20 minutes.

2. Wrap closely in plastic wrap, then put in a tightly closed container and store for months in the refrigerator. When ready to use, bring to room temperature and knead again. If marzipan is too stiff, knead in a drop or two of warmed corn syrup until original consistency is restored. Yield 1⅓ pounds or enough for four figures.

❄ How to work with marzipan

Marzipan is easy to tint. Break off a portion of the batch and knead in liquid food color, a drop at a time, until you reach the tint desired. To tint brown, knead in cocoa. For a rich, appetizing tan, knead in dry instant coffee powder.

To roll out marzipan, dust work surface and a small rolling pin with a sifting of confectioners' sugar. Work with a small portion at a time. Roll out just like cookie or pie dough. Cut the rolled marzipan with small cookie cutters or gum paste cutters, or use a small sharp knife.

Use egg white as glue to attach one piece of marzipan to another. Lightly stir the egg white in a small container. Dip or brush egg white on one piece and attach to second piece with a turning motion.

Always glaze completed fruits or figures as soon as they have dried enough to hold their shapes. Besides giving the pieces an attractive gloss, the glaze will keep the marzipan fresh and moist.

CORN SYRUP GLAZE
    ½ cup light corn syrup
    1 cup water

Combine syrup and water and heat to boiling in a small saucepan. Brush on marzipan while hot. Allow to dry at room temperature, about 20 minutes. This will give a soft shine to the figures.

For a shinier finish, substitute just one tablespoon of water for the one cup of water in the recipe.

❄ How to model figures in marzipan

All marzipan figures are made from combinations of basic forms—balls, rounded cones and cylinders. Shape the marzipan between your palms like modeling clay, attach the pieces and add details—you've created a real little personality!

Trims and details are usually cut from rolled marzipan. Small cutters, a sharp knife and decorating tubes make this work go quickly.

❄ Estimate amounts needed and tint

Make a recipe of marzipan and divide into portions for various tints. For Santa, Mrs. Santa and the two elves in the picture on page 12, divide this way:

1. Cut off a very small amount to leave untinted.

2. Form remainder of marzipan into a large cylinder. Cut off about one-eighth of it to tint brown. Cut off another eighth to tint flesh color.

3. From remainder of cylinder, cut off one-third to tint red. Tint the rest of the marzipan green.

4. Keep marzipan tightly wrapped in plastic until you are ready to model it.

❄ Work in orderly progression

1. *A day ahead,* form ball for head, cone for body and U-shaped cylinder for legs. Form feet, if needed, and dry overnight on wax paper.

2. *Next day,* form cylinder for arms. Attach rolled marzipan trims. Now join feet, legs and body. Add arms, then head. Complete with features, hair and final details. Dry on wax paper for about an hour, then glaze.

Actual-size diagrams for marzipan figures on page 12

SANTA CLAUS

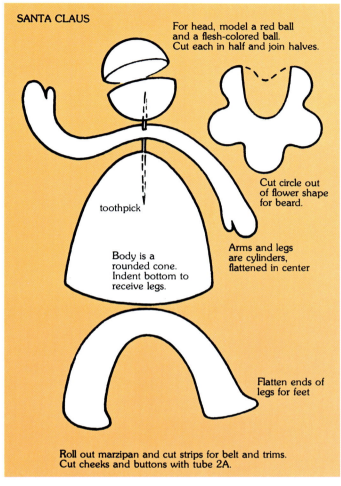

For head, model a red ball and a flesh-colored ball. Cut each in half and join halves.

Cut circle out of flower shape for beard.

Arms and legs are cylinders, flattened in center

Body is a rounded cone. Indent bottom to receive legs.

toothpick

Flatten ends of legs for feet

Roll out marzipan and cut strips for belt and trims. Cut cheeks and buttons with tube 2A.

MRS. CLAUS

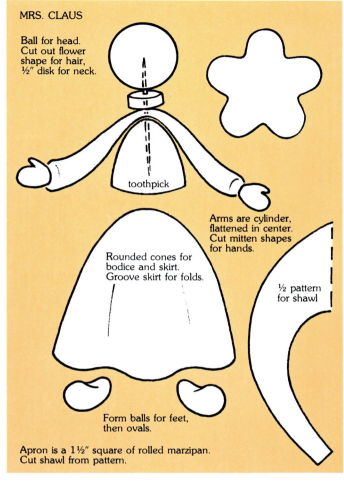

Ball for head. Cut out flower shape for hair, ½" disk for neck.

toothpick

Arms are cylinder, flattened in center. Cut mitten shapes for hands.

Rounded cones for bodice and skirt. Groove skirt for folds.

½ pattern for shawl

Form balls for feet, then ovals.

Apron is a 1½" square of rolled marzipan. Cut shawl from pattern.

ELF FIGURES

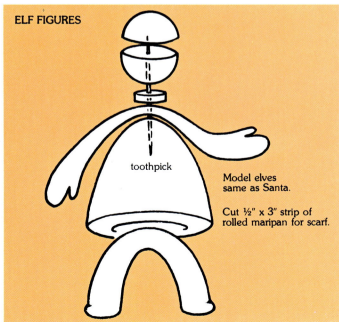

toothpick

Model elves same as Santa.

Cut ½" x 3" strip of rolled maripan for scarf.

MAIL BOX

MAIL BOX
Form a cylinder and flatten as shown here. Mount on candy cane.

side view

front view

SANTA'S SACK
Cut a 5" circle from rolled marzipan. Wrap around three marshmallows.

Tested recipes for cookies, candy, icing

Grandma's gingerbread

Delicious, very easy to put together and rolls out smoothly. The baked dough is strong and rigid to support the weight of candy and icing trims.

    5 cups all-purpose flour (approximate)
    1 teaspoon baking soda
    1 teaspoon salt
    2 teaspoons ginger
    2 teaspoons cinnamon
    1 teaspoon nutmeg
    1 teaspoon cloves
    1 cup solid white vegetable shortening
    1 cup sugar
    1¼ cups unsulphured molasses
    2 eggs, beaten

1. Thoroughly blend flour, soda, salt and spices. Melt shortening in large saucepan. Add sugar, molasses, and eggs; mix well. Cool, then add four cups of the blended dry ingredients and mix well. Preheat oven to 350°F.

2. Turn mixture onto lightly floured surface. Knead in remaining dry ingredients by hand. Add a little more flour, if necessary, to make a firm dough.

3. Roll out dough on the backs of lightly oiled cookie sheets as page 6 describes. Time baking according to thickness of rolled dough. For large pieces, ⅛″ thick, bake as long as fourteen minutes. For smaller pieces, rolled thinly, six or seven minutes may be enough. Check frequently to avoid over-browning. Remove from cookie sheets to wire racks with a large spatula. Cool about 30 minutes. Then cover a flat surface with paper toweling and place baked pieces on it to dry overnight.

4. Wrap unused dough tightly in plastic wrap and refrigerate to keep for weeks. Bring to room temperature and knead briefly to use again. Yield: enough for any of the projects in this book with some left over for cookies.

Roll-out cookies

This recipe makes a delicious firm cookie that holds its shape and tints easily.

    1¼ cups butter
    2 cups sugar
    2 eggs
    5 cups all-purpose flour (approximate)
    1 teaspoon baking powder
    1 teaspoon salt
    1 teaspoon grated orange peel
    ½ cup milk

1. Cream butter and sugar together, then add eggs and beat until fluffy. Sift dry ingredients together and add alternately to creamed mixture with milk.

2. Turn out on lightly floured surface. Knead in more flour as necessary to make a firm dough. To tint, knead in paste food

color applied with a toothpick until you reach the color you wish. Refrigerate, wrapped tightly in plastic wrap for about an hour before rolling out.

3. Preheat oven to 325°F. Roll out on back of lightly oiled cookie sheets to ⅛″ thickness, just as described on page 6. Use a lightly floured rolling pin.

4. Bake about 12 minutes, checking frequently so edges do not brown. Remove immediately to wire racks to cool for about 30 minutes, then lay pieces on a flat surface covered with paper towels to dry overnight.

5. Wrap any unused dough tightly in plastic wrap and refrigerate for weeks. Bring to room temperature and knead briefly to use again. Yield: about four dozen large cookies.

Wilton royal icing—meringue

Use as "glue" to assemble structures, and for piping decorative trims. Beat with a stationary electric mixer. Fast drying— keep bowl covered with a damp cloth.

    3 tablespoons meringue powder
    3½ ounces warm water
    1 pound confectioners' sugar, sifted
    ½ teaspoon cream of tartar

1. Combine ingredients, mixing slowly, then beat at high speed for 7 to 10 minutes. For piping fine trims, thin with light corn syrup—about one teaspoon per cup of icing.

2. Store leftover icing, tightly covered, in the refrigerator for weeks. Rebeat before using again. Yield: about 3½ cups—more than enough for any project in this book.

Boiled icing—meringue

This icing makes a perfect glistening "snow", very easy to stroke on. Keep utensils grease-free—grease will break down. Use a stationary electric mixer.

Mixture One:
    2 cups granulated sugar
    ½ cup warm water
    ¼ teaspoon cream of tartar
Mixture Two:
    ½ cup warm water
    4 tablespoons meringue powder
    3½ cups sifted confectioners' sugar
    ¼ cup white corn syrup

1. Combine ingredients in Mixture One in a 1½-quart heavy saucepan. Place over high heat and stir until all sugar crystals are dissolved. After this, do not stir. Insert candy thermometer and wash down with a pastry brush dipped in hot water. Wash down sides of pan twice more as mixture cooks. At 240°F, remove from heat.

2. Meanwhile, prepare Mixture Two. Whip meringue powder and water about seven

minutes or until fluffy. Add confectioners' sugar and whip at low speed about three minutes. Slowly pour hot syrup (Mixture One) into batch and whip at high speed until light and very fluffy. Now add the corn syrup and whip about three minutes. Use immediately or refrigerate in a tightly closed container for weeks. Bring to room temperature rebeat to use again.

3. Before using, test consistency of icing. Add a little additional corn syrup if needed for easy spreadability. Yield: about six cups, enough for any project in this book.

Hard candy

One of the quickest and easiest candies you can make! Be sure to use molds designed for high temperatures. And cook in a heavy saucepan, no more than two-quart capacity.

    1 cup granulated cane sugar
    ⅓ cup hot water
    ⅓ cup light corn syrup
    ½ teaspoon liquid food color
    ½ teaspoon *oil-based* flavoring

1. Lightly brush ten small lollipop molds, or other heat-proof molds with vegetable oil. Assemble on oiled cookie sheet.

2. Combine sugar, hot water and corn syrup in a heavy saucepan. Place on high heat and stir with a wooden spoon until all sugar crystals are dissolved. Wash down sides of pan with a pastry brush dipped in hot water. Clip on thermometer. Continue cooking, without stirring, to 290°F, then remove from heat. Entire cooking process takes about nine minutes.

3. Add flavoring and food color and stir to blend. Pour into prepared molds. Let harden at room temperature about ten minutes. Unmold and lay on a paper towel to absorb oil. When completely cool, wrap tightly in plastic wrap until ready to use. Store at room temperature up to six weeks. Yield: ten 2″ lollipops, or about 15 small molded shapes.

Sugar molds

    2 cups granulated sugar
    1 teaspoon liquid food coloring
    3 teaspoons egg white, lightly stirred

1. Place sugar in bowl, add food coloring and egg white and knead with your hands until well blended. Pack firmly into mold and level top with a spatula. Cover mold with cardboard, turn over and lift mold off. (For sparkle, immediately dust with edible glitter.)

2. Dry thoroughly, about five hours. For a large hollow mold, place in 200°F oven five minutes. Carefully tip sugar mold into your palm and scoop out damp sugar inside with a teaspoon. Replace on cardboard and dry thoroughly about 24 hours. Yield: two large sugar molds.